All those memories!!

Anneline

PARIAN CHRONICLES

FOREIGN AFFAIRS WITH A GREEK ISLAND

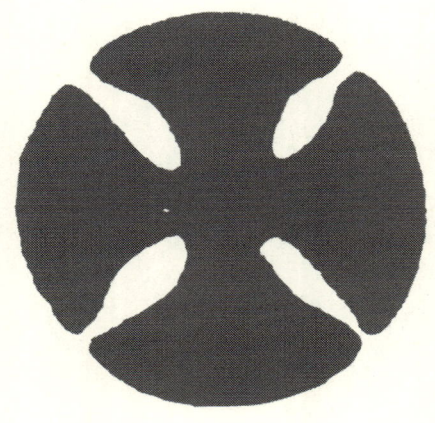

COMPILED BY
FIONNUALA BRENNAN
&
CHARLOTTE CARLIN

INDEX

Preface   4

Robin Brown, 1965   9
Florence Tamburro, 1966   31
Phillada Lecomte, 1968   40
Deirdre Grieve, 1969   62
Sabine Grootendorst, 1969   74
Irene Grootendorst, 1969   86
Annelize Goedbloed, 1972   104
Gregorio Altamirano, 1973   124
Alexandra Senfft, 1974   136
Patricia Donnelly, 1976   146
Mary Bilz & Bert Jones, 1977   154
Fionnuala Brennan, 1977   164
Charlotte Carlin, 1984   180
Jean Polyzoides, 1985   198
Gail Saunders, 1985   212
Suzanne Rolland, 1987   224

PREFACE

One day **one** and the **other** went for a walk. **One** asked the **other** about her Paros story, about when, how and why she had come to the island. The **other** answered and when she had finished, said: *You know what; I've often toyed with the idea of interviewing people for a book about just that. Since that is the question we all ask of each other, why not put it into writing? And you know what?* The **one** replied, a few years back *I sent out a questionnaire to all the foreigners I could think of and asked them the questions I've just asked you. So, why don't you fill in that questionnaire?*

The **other** did. She filled in when the when and from where, but when she came to how and why she realized that *that* was going to take more than just a few moments, so she went back to her home country and wrote her story. When **one** and the **other** met up again, the **other** suggested that they contact all these people again, whom **one** had contacted all those years ago, and ask them if they would be interested in writing their own story, which **one** and the **other** would then assemble into a compilation of stories, to be published as a non-profit e-book for ourselves, friends and families. And that is just what one and the other have done!

We had no intention of reaching a big market. This is a collection of personal stories about the writers' early days on Paros. Most of us came here in the 1960s, 70s and 80s. Our stories celebrate an island which had yet to experience the tsunami of mass tourism and the effects of modernisation: of tarred roads, of electricity, of running water, of big supermarkets; of fancy clothes shops and chic bars, nightclubs and restaurants; of swimming pools and garden centres; of mobile phones, internet cafes and computer shops. Our stories are, to some extent, une recherche du temps perdu. The stories are also an attempt to tell each other what we value so much about Paros and her people. The book is an expression of gratitude to Parians and to Paros for the warm welcome we continue to experience here.

We have contacted as many people as we could think of who came to the island during those decades. We contacted more than sixty people, whom we either knew personally, knew of, were referred to, or who, having heard of our project, contacted us. Everybody was welcome as long as they would submit their stories in English. The only criterion for contributing has been people's wish to do so, not whether they were 'professional' writers or not.

In terms of 'editing' all we have done is proofread the stories for spelling and punctuation. As for the non-native English speakers' stories, we have left some different ways of expressing things which, while not strictly correct in English, are easily understandable as they are, thus preserving the original 'tone' of their respective languages (Danish, Dutch, French and German). With regard to the spelling of Greek place names, we have not striven for consistency, as there is no really correct way in English, given that Greek has different letters.

We have, otherwise, not acted as editors, but rather as compilers. We have encouraged people to write, but we have not given advice, nor have we asked people to cut or add to their stories.

This is not, of course, the full story. No doubt there are still many foreigners here who have their stories, which they might like to share. They may wish to take up the thread and weave another homage to Paros.

Although every single story is in essence a proclamation of love for Paros, we, the compilers, still wish to state that we cannot be held responsible for the content of any story other than our own.

Finally, we wish to express our thanks to everybody who took up the gauntlet and agreed to share not only their stories, but also their family photos with us. Thanks also to Robin Brown for so generously sharing his experiences with self-publishing, to Deirdre Grieve for coming up with just the right title, to Peter Macken for converting all our old photos into a printable size and, not least, for designing the beautiful front cover. Ultimately, we want to thank Orla Brennan and Keith Doyle for adding the final embellishing touches to the layout of the book.

Fionnuala Brennan and Charlotte Carlin

ROBIN'S STORY · 1965
By Robin Brown

Robin as minstrel

The early years

Our rented bikes bumped off the edge of the tarmac, and came down on the earth track at the top of the hill. Before us in the distance was Naoussa; two miles behind us lay Paroikia, where we had arrived the previous evening. The Apollon was too big to approach the fishermen's quay, and we were brought ashore with a handful of others by a small taxi-boat. Apart from during high summer, a single ship called at Paros on alternate days in 1965. "Paros: nice looking island, smiling and tender; with its deeply notched shores going down to the sea, seeming to welcome the strange with love." So said the tourist pamphlet. The French section had said "Nous allons chaque jour à Antiparos dans un petit benzine gateau." Already we were charmed. We pedalled hard downhill against the wind, and sometime later we arrived dusty and thirsty in the centre of the then small village of Naoussa, beyond the stream. It was after lunchtime. Only two restaurants were to be found. The zacharoplastaeo simply had cream cones and thick coffee. At the small taverna opposite I tried the Greek from the back pages of the Michelin Guide. "Ti eketai na fai?" A cheerful woman served us the ochra and tomato stew she had prepared for the family. We were hungry: in spite of the glutinous texture, it tasted good. We wandered around the little fishing harbour, and explored the winding alleys and tunnels behind it. Then we pushed our bikes over the hill, headed for the beach to the east, and swam.

From the town around to Ay. Maria headland we had the whole bay to ourselves, except for one man half-a-mile away. After a while, he wandered down and introduced himself:

a German student, travelling around like us. We compared notes - where had we been? where was he going? "Next I go to Santorini, to see my house." A student had a house on Santorini? "Yes, it only cost us 400 DM a few years ago." What?! Even we, hard up and renting our flat, could lay hands on 400 DM. "Of course, it was not a very good house. It only had three walls, and no roof.
But it was somewhere to spread our sleeping bags, and cheaper than the hotel.
We bought it between four of us. Now I go back to see if it is still there."

There was a clip-clop sound behind the dry-stone wall. It was the grape harvest; everywhere donkeys and mules, loaded with large panniers, were carrying their precious cargoes to the wineries and treading pits. "Wait here a moment". Quickly he returned with an armful of beautiful grapes - pale pink, veined with red, and toasted gold on the side towards the sun. They burst and melted in our mouths, as we knelt in the marble sand. "What do we owe you?" we asked. "Nothing. I offered, but the donkey-man said they were a gift. The harvest was good." We were young, and falling in love again - this time with an island. Somewhere at the back of my mind, an idea was beginning to form.

In Paroikia next morning we went to the Information Office in the windmill, beside the port. "Are there any houses for sale?" Christos - maybe seventeen, but speaking fair English - consulted with Roula. Quietly, they closed the office. "No matter; it's the last day anyway, and no customers all week". "I know two houses are selling. But not very good - they are quite broken." An understatement indeed. Both houses were in the back street of the town. One was simply a hole between two houses: the other still boasted the remains of the first floor. Neither was anywhere near the sea. "Is not expensive... maybe", offered Christos, a little crestfallen. But the idea had taken root. "Is it expensive to build a house?" I asked. "Ah, you must meet my friend. He is a builder." Enter Giorgos. That evening at the Asteria - a long-vanished garden restaurant on the Agora -

the first sketches were made on a paper table-napkin. Giovanna was singing 'Y Myrtia', and the perfume of night jasmine hung on the air.

Donkeys

We were sitting one evening in Giorgos' yard under the vines by the Naoussa road. A rarity – a car - passed by. "Are there many cars on Paros? I asked. Giorgos said "Yes, many – I think seven." Times have changed. Negotiations went on for ages to buy a site that Giorgos had found. There were difficulties, as it depended on a farmer getting to town to transfer the land to his daughter, who was willing to sell a site to us. But the farmer's donkey was sick, and unable to carry him to town. At that time, once you were off the few tarmacked roads, the only practical transport over the rocky paths was either by donkey or by mule; and the few year-round expatriates treasured their donkeys if they were lucky enough to have one. Eventually the donkey recovered, and in 1967 we came back to Paros to sign the purchase deed. Giorgo's correspondence was written for him in English by Dick Lethen, and during that time we became good friends. He was our first contact with The Aegean School of Arts, and we have remained friends with them down the years.

It was in one of those early visits that the 31st of August fell on a Sunday; so that became the obvious end of the tourist season. The Meltemi had rampaged for weeks. All the visitors packed onto the evening ferry and returned to Piraeus. And, most unusually, there was a sharp rainstorm. Next morning was calm and beautiful. Such crowds as Paros attracted in those days had vanished; the Athenians had gone home, the summer dust was laid, and the air was crystal clear: it seemed as if you could simply reach out and touch Sifnos and Serifos. Walking into the town we met Vasilly, Giorgos' brother. "Doxe se o These" he said – "Thanks be to God" "Why?", I asked. "Because summer is over. Now we can relax, and enjoy some good weather and good company again!"

Reflections on Grape juice

A few days later I was walking along past the old generator hall, (which later became the incredibly noisy Mirevolos discotheque). The ancient diesel engines rumbled day and night to supply the whole island with electricity. As in most remote communities, everyone kept candles and matches ready for the frequent blackouts. Walking along in a daydream, I tripped on a big pipe, and almost went flying. I looked up to see Vasilly; he was laughing at me. Then I looked down at the pipe: it was thick like a fire-hose, and black. It snaked across the yard, and then the road, and plunged into the sea. In the middle of the bay a small tanker lay at anchor, and I thought I could see the pipe climbing up the side of the ship. In the other direction the pipe ran to a big old International tractor chuntering gently driving a pump, and behind that it climbed into a large concrete tank. This was in the donkey yard in front of the old Agricultural Co-Operative warehouse; a part of which - with a few touches of whitewash - has become The Archilocos Concert Hall on the waterfront by the fishing port. "Whatever is happening?" I asked. "That's our wine" replied Vasilly. "The grape harvest is in two weeks. We have to empty the tanks for the new wine." As a Swiss resident at the time, who fondly imagined he knew about wine, I was appalled at the thought of wine being pumped from a concrete vat to a tanker-ship in a fire hose! "But whoever buys *that*?" "That ship is going to Marseilles. The poor French, with their weak sun and cold climate, cannot make wine with enough sugar and alcohol to keep through even one winter." I choked! "So they buy our strong wine, and add it to theirs, so that it will keep till next year. Another ship will come at New Year, and that one goes to Genoa."

It was several years later that a French research student accidentally, and embarrassingly, confirmed every word that I had been told, and much more. She had found the isotopic signature of *mineral* carbon in French Appellation Controlé wine! The subsequent inquiry blamed the Spaniards, who were supposed to supply wine alcohol to reinforce the cheapest Bordeaux. "Travail à l'anglais" was what the French called it! But the Spaniards had used all their cheap spirit on their own wine, and instead sold mineral alcohol to the French. This brought to light the fact that this 'marque de distinction', AC, was only obliged to contain 70% of wine from the region; the remainder could consist of the strong rich wines from North Africa and – yes – Greece. This was news to all of Europe; the scandal was promptly christened 'Winegate' by the Herald Tribune. But when I had heard the truth on Paros years previously, I could not believe my ears!

Our introduction to island wine had happened first on Syros. In a dark little café behind the port in Ermopoulis a lovely old lady, speaking elegant French and shaped like a pyramid, served us two small glasses. "We call it Black Wine" she said, "And it is so strong we usually drink it with water." It was black as the night, but so rich and sweet that it tasted like liquid sunshine! That was our introduction to Mavro. Forty years ago it was the only wine you could find on the islands; it was too sweet for meals, but we grew to love it for the warm glow it bestowed. Nowadays you can only find it from a very few suppliers, who mostly tread it themselves. The best used to come from Marathi.

Early in our summers on Paros our neighbours, the Kalakonas family, organised a grape treading in their lower field. (The treading pit is still there, in the Blue Lounge floor, to this day.) The grapes were picked in big wicker baskets, and simply tipped into the large pit, which had been freshly whitewashed a few days before. Then everyone rolled up their trousers to the knee, and joined in squishing the grapes to a mush. We and our daughters were invited to join in. We waded into the sea afterwards to rinse off the purple juice. I have never seen so many wasps in one place before, but no one got stung.

There was much hilarity and drinking off the previous years wine, served together with little hot sausages cooked on an open grill. The juice from the grapes was strained through an opening to a lower pit; this opening was largely blocked by a large fragrant thyme bush – plucked roots and all from the headland -, which served as a strainer to hold back the must and the grape skins. The filtered juice was then poured into a large wineskin. This was huge, a whole cowhide sewn sides-to-middle, with the seams sealed with pitch. Pine resin was used to seal skins used for white wine, which gave the distinctive flavour to Retsina. I had been speculating on the economics of farming in the islands, and I supposed that this was probably their cash crop. When I asked Giorgos Kalakonas when they were going to sell it, at first he didn't understand my question. When finally the drachma dropped, he roared with laughter. "Sell it? *Sell our wine?!*" We're going to drink it – all of it!" With that, he picked up the whole skin, hoisted it to his shoulder, and carried it alone up to the farmhouse. It must have weighed over a hundred kilos.

Spring

One year we had the good fortune to arrive on Paros during the spring. Summer visitors can well have the impression that the Cyclades are always the colour of golden toast, with occasional evergreens. But this is only their summer costume, when in the heat most of the grasses and many of the trees go into suspended animation. But spring in Greece is brief and blindingly beautiful. One problem is that you can never book it in advance, because you never know precisely enough when it is going to happen – it may be early in March, or it may be at the end of May, and it will last only a few short weeks. When the days become warmer, the grass becomes as green as in an Alpine meadow. And it is covered with miniature flowers – perfect irises only an inch high, or gentians and tiny narcissi. The first flowers of spring are usually the everlasting flowers, then in

the freshwater streambeds come large lupines in big indigo clusters. Cherry and apple blossoms deck the orchards high up the mountain at Aghios Ioannis Kaparis.
The mezembrianthemums burst into their scarlet and sky blue flowers from their dark green succulent creepers on the stone walls and beside the rocky paths, followed in turn by a multitude of jasmine, orange blossom, roses and many other flowering bushes in gardens. The tiny blue flowers on the thyme bushes reflect the azure of the Cycladic skies above the Krotiri headland, which is so highly perfumed that you can smell it for a sea mile downwind. Then, as the heat tightens its grip on the island, you will notice one day that the grasses look less fresh. And the next day it is all over. The flowers vanish except in the gardens, and green disappears from the landscape until the rains return in the autumn.

Within two weeks the corn will be harvested. When we first arrived on Paros it was mostly cut by hand. The sheaves of corn were thrown onto threshing circles of beaten earth or cement, where it was trampled usually by a pair of animals roped together and dragging a heavy wooden beam to shake the ears of corn from the stalks. This was then tossed in the air, so that the growing north wind could winnow out the lighter chaff and carry it away downwind, so that the now cleaned grain could be bagged for storage. Paros used to have many windmills to grind the corn, but they had fallen into disuse before our arrival.

The End of the Beginning

Giorgo met us off the evening ferry. It was four years since the whole project had started. We checked our bags into the Hotel Kypreou, in the 'Square' opposite the big church. We had intended to go to see the house by daylight, but Giorgo was impatient to show us his new creation. (Years later, he once said "All my houses are really like my children.") So, with our little girl in our arms, we set off around the bay. And we stood gasping in amazement as Giorgo, almost hugging himself with pride, showed us by the light of a primus lamp the first of 'Ta Anglika Spitia'. Ours.....really? Well - not quite. Although the Parians know us well enough, they call the house 'Giorgo's House' to this day

Afterthought

Translation between Greek and English is tricky at the best of times. Typos and spelling errors abound: some are even lovingly preserved. Porkohops and Gordon Elue went through at least three printings of the Dionysos menu; "the customers expect it", the patron explained. Idioms are even trickier.

But.... *'the strange with love'*..... that, dear reader.... was us.

Robin Brown.
Sauverny, France.
February 2012.

Note: This essay is based on a shorter article, which appeared in Paros Life in July 2004 entitled 'Strange with Love'. It is incorporated here with the permission of the Editor, Vicky Pres

A week to remember
By Robin Brown

The midday ferry arrived in the bay with its siren sounding all the way from Aghios Fokas headland, and it went blasting on for the whole hour it was at the town dock. It was Saturday the 20th of July 1974. Greece was mobilising, calling up all the army reservists. We were not sure quite what this would mean for us, in the middle of a fortnight's holiday on Paros with two little girls of four and six years old; now we suddenly found ourselves halfway between two countries on the brink of war.

The military dictatorship had seized power in Athens seven years previously, just months after we had laid our plans to build a summer home on Paros. During the previous winter we had come on a hardworking sabbatical year, and brought the family to live in Aghia Paraskevi – then still the last green suburb on the edge of Athens. It was a fascinating opportunity to get to know Greece better. All civil rights had long been suspended, though I hoped that my semi-diplomatic visitor status would protect us. But the visit felt ominous from the beginning: I stepped out of my taxi, and stood straight on a fired rifle shell. This was three days after the military police had crushed a student radio rebellion at the Polytechnion in Athens, killing eighty-three according to foreign journalists at the time. (A military inquiry gave very different figures.) Greece had generally put up with 'the regime' up to that point. In the countryside and the islands the farmers and fishermen had benefited from subsidies, and there was still some support for the Colonels. But the military had killed 'The Children of Athens', and the mood there was of sullen hatred for everyone in a uniform. The military police toured Athens in patrols of a dozen men, wearing Marlon Brando type dark glasses, and glowering at people on the sidewalks from the saddles of their white Harleys. The civil police felt so unsafe that they changed out of their uniforms at work, and walked home in pairs while the citizens of Athens jeered, singing the choruses of banned songs by Theodorakis. We lived close to one of the many military tank depots that ringed the city: all the guns faced downtown. There was no doubt that the Colonels felt they were defending Greece against the Athenians. We had left Athens to get away from this nightmare atmosphere. A couple of weeks on peaceful Paros had become necessary for our spirits.

On that fateful Saturday morning we had come down for breakfast as usual, in our alcove overlooking Livadia bay. I turned on the radio to check on political developments, as I was worried that this holiday on the island might become untenable. The Greek military government had supported a sudden coup five days earlier against the very political Archbishop Makarios, who was the President of Cyprus, forcing Makarios to flee for his life. The previous day their underground movement EOKA had installed a replacement as President. EOKA firmly intended to bring about Enosis – or union with Greece; the military hoped that this would restore them some credit in the eyes of the Greek people. But obviously, given recent history, this would be strongly opposed by the scattered Turkish communities on Cyprus, amounting to one fifth of the population. The probable reaction of Turkey was not in doubt, the only question was its timing. We got the BBC direct from Cyprus on the shortwave 49-metre band, and the news was alarming in the extreme. "This morning before dawn Turkish planes attacked defence positions around Kyrenia in Northern Cyprus, and troop and tank landings started at first light. Fighting with the Cyprus defence forces is continuing at several positions around the Kyreneia peninsula, and bombs are reported to have fallen near Nicosia". The rest of the news was that the chancelleries of Europe had reacted like a stirred ants nest. Then at nine o'clock the BBC went off the air, and we were left until evening without any news except Greek, and that appeared to be just broadcasting martial music and national folksongs. Now what were we going to do?

The ferry Elli had left, and we heard later that nearly all the men aged up to thirty-five who had served in the armed forces had left with it. All the ships had been sailing for years with sealed orders, to be opened in case of an emergency. An uneasy silence returned to the harbour. We went over to the town in our little boat 'Soysmanda' – an invented name derived from our two daughters – and tied up in the fishermen's port, which was then on the edge of Paroikia town. We walked into town. But although it was a Saturday morning, all the shops appeared shut, and very few people were about. We walked along the deserted waterfront, wondering how a beautiful blue and sunny morning could suddenly feel sinister, until we came to the little square halfway along the sea front. Both Dionysi Ventouri's café, and the 'Glass Café' opposite, were open; a few people sat at the tables. Dionysi was an old friend of ours – he had served us our very first breakfast on Paros one early morning nine years previously. I wandered in to order our usual "dhio Ness' me gala, kai dhia pagota". He looked at me sadly, and shook his head. "Dhen einai kali nea". I asked him what he thought would happen? He tossed his head back, shrugged his shoulders, and said nothing. Beside him on the counter was a photo of his son in uniform, holding up a large automatic pistol. This sort of thing was necessary in those days as a silent declaration in favour of the military – even from probably the kindest and best loved man on the island. Over the last few years the photographs in all the shops, which used to be of moustachioed grandfathers and founders of the business, were gradually replaced by shots of owners or relatives in military uniforms.

I tried to gather some news from the TV in cafes, with little success. Few people seemed interested in fact, as it was always the same – Colonels at prizegivings at primary schools, Generals opening new roads, Brigadiers addressing silent rows of secondary students, and so on. Beyond a short statement that the Turks were attacking Cyprus, and that Greece had called up the army reservists, there was no news on the actual developments to be had. The Greek radio and television news were heavily censored; home news was only propaganda, and international news was mostly slanted and usually several days late. Besides, although by then I was fairly fluent in Demotiki Greek, the news was in Katherevousa, and I could only partly understand it. We returned to the house, took the girls to the beach, and waited impatiently until the short wave came back in the evening. A small ship came into the harbour without fuss, unloaded some cargo onto the quay, and left rapidly and silently. When we could receive the BBC, we learned that the Cypriot troops had initially had some success, and were holding the Turks penned around Kyrenia. But bombing around and in Nicosia was becoming heavier. I heard later from friends in Athens that the mobilisation had caused chaos: businesses stopped for lack of staff, and transport – buses and taxis – largely stopped for lack of drivers. The ports handled the arriving multitudes well enough, but the reservists who had to report to the Northern Army in Thessaly had to drive there by their own means. Which would probably have worked – except that the air force had taken over three large straight sections of the National Road to use as emergency aerodromes! The nascent army reinforcements were bumping over cornfields in their requisitioned Mini Minors and Mercedes taxis. Meanwhile on Paros, the first night of the Cyprus Crisis passed quietly.

The Sunday morning news on the BBC was much more alarming. It was not a news broadcast at all, but a direct address to everyone – Greeks Turks and foreigners alike – in northern Cyprus. "Two military convoys will be leaving the British sovereign base areas at 0900 hours. They will call in turn at all the villages, towns and resorts along the north coast of Cyprus, including those where hostilities are taking place. Their mission is to collect all British citizens, and any other foreign nationals who desire our protection, and to transport them to safe areas prior to repatriation. This mission is a humanitarian operation, and will not fire on the combatants. However the convoys are under armed protection, and will defend themselves if attacked." In other words, it would only take a Cypriot soldier who had not heard the news, or an EOKA hothead making trouble, and Britain could be involved in a three-way shooting war. The same broadcast was heard by a close friend of mine, who had been by the sea in Cyprus; and who had spent the last twenty four hours in a hotel basement with only water from the radiator circuit to drink, sheltering from strafing raids by Turkish fighters. Another more recent friend told me she was also sheltering in a hotel basement; teenage Turkish boy soldiers burst in and machine-gunned over the heads of the tourists and Greeks inside. There were many wounded all around her. The survivors were rescued by the convoys and taken to HMS Hermes, and later flown to Britain from the base area in the south near Larnaca.

A little later Vassily – our builder's brother - called by: "Robin, what do you know about what is happening? What is really going on? The news tells us nothing, but they have called up all the army reservists. Who are we fighting – the Turks? The Cypriots? The British? What does the BBC say? I know you have a special radio." Briefly, I told him the little I knew. He listened intently, then said "Deutch Welle says the Americans are pressuring the Colonels not to do anything more in Cyprus." I could well believe it. It seems an ex-gästarbeiter who lived up the mountain also had a short wave receiver; as did a reputed communist near Naoussa, who listened every night to Radio Moscow. The only international news on Paros that Sunday came from we three, with listening ears for the outside world – at least by night. Vassily said "You saw that second ship that came yesterday – do you know what it was bringing? Rifles! The older reservists who remained here have to organise the defence of the island. Are we at war?" On Sunday evening the news appeared to be that the northern army was ordered to prepare for a Turkish invasion – or outright war. No ship at all came to Paros on Sunday.

On Monday morning the news was confused: before we lost the short wave at nine o'clock it was unclear what was happening in Athens, and what the army's orders were. On the far side of the anchorage, in front of the Apollon Hotel, there was an old Brixham trawler flying the British Blue Ensign; the skipper was an ex-Royal Navy man. I took the boat over and hailed him, and he invited me on board. "I knew I shouldn't stay here", he said. "But I thought I had a bit more time, and now here I am – stuck". Him and me, both! I asked where he had intended to go. "Turkey of course: with odds of sixty to eight million, who do you think is going to lose this war the colonels want to start? I know a sheltered bay, inaccessible from the shore; I'd have waited there till it's safe to come out. But it's too late now!" He had an all-band short wave receiver: I resolved to get one myself as soon as possible. But even on the higher frequencies we could not get better information at midday.

I heard the real story of that day on our eventual return to Athens. Unlike the account given in Wikipedia, attributing it to negotiations between various politicians in Athens, the fact of the matter is that the Northern Army – which still harboured a number of royalist officers facing the front line in a totally unnecessary war – rebelled. On Sunday they sent an open letter to the military government, and copied it to all the newspapers, accusing the colonels' regime of usurpation and betrayal of Greece. They announced that they were sending an armoured column to Athens, whose mission would be to arrest all members of the military government they could find, on a charge of high treason. And this they proceeded to do. The only member of the government who came to work on that Monday was the infamous Brigadier Ioannides, he who had ordered the storming of the Polytechnion. This was the reason for the confusion in the news reports – the military government had simply evaporated. That evening the BBC carried the news. We were vastly relieved, as were nearly all the ex-patriates living on Paros. I think it was Paulien Lethen who told me "It was marvellous news! We came running down from our house, telling everyone we met 'isn't it great? The government has fallen – we are all free again!' But every Greek we spoke to just fell silent, and looked worried or afraid. They all hurried home without a word." I suppose that a deeply conservative people, most of whom had endured the Second World War and then the Civil War which followed it, and who had lived in a beautiful but relatively poor place for almost all of their lives, viewed any change at all to the established order as being most likely a change for the worse. At the very least it probably meant new rules, new accommodations with new authorities, probably new expenses, and most likely the loss of the subsidies, which had eased their recent years. Why should they be pleased too?

But the Turks were not to be so easily pacified. The international news on the Tuesday had ominous rumours of Turkish reinforcements manoeuvring on the western coasts and towards the Greek frontier zone. After a short setback, over three days they had advanced as far as Nicosia in Cyprus, and thousands of Greek Cypriots fled south towards safety in the central mountains, leaving forever their homes on the fertile plains of the north. The Colonels had unleashed EOKA, and provoked Turkey to the point of war. The northern army had brought down the military government, but now it looked as if the Turks might have their war anyway. There had been no passenger ships since last Friday. I asked around about ships. I was told, "Yes, a ship is coming tonight." Cars were already gathering at the dock. The only two ferries, which served Paros, the Elli and the Kyklades, carried a maximum of thirty-nine and thirty-five cars respectively. It looked hopeless, as there were already over fifty cars waiting.

Meanwhile we were running very low on supplies. We went into town again. Although a few tourist shops were open, all the essential grocers shops appeared shut. At the well-known crossroads at the bottom of the Agora four shops – famous in their time – faced each other. In their respective corners they were 'O Piratis' a grocer, the cobbler, one of the Frangoulis pharmacies, and 'The Brothers' Adonis and Giorgos Theokarides grocers shop. Adonis saw us through the window, and cracked open the door to let us in. Like all the grocers he was rationing supplies to regular customers only, to avoid panic buying and empty shelves. We saw why at the pharmacy: a woman was desperately buying up all the under-arm deodorant she could carry!

I noticed a curious thing on this day. The Greek TV news was broadcasting the real truth, only half a day after the international news had already sent it out. It looked as if they had submitted it to the censors' office, but the censors had all gone home, so after a while they went ahead and broadcast it anyway. And *nobody on the island would believe it.* They kept asking me "What does the BBC say? Deutch Welle says ... etc etc." This is the ultimate refutation of media censorship – when you *do* tell the truth, no one believes you!

I took our old Opel to town and parked it on the quay: it was sixty ninth in the queue. Not a chance! Around two in the morning I heard a ship drop its anchors with a huge rattle of chains. I looked at my watch, thought of getting everyone up for nothing; then I thought 'Oh what the hell!' turned over, and went back to sleep. I woke again at four; I could still hear the ship's engines. 'That's odd', I thought, 'but it's too late now'. Next morning the Opel was alone on the dock. In the Paros dust on the back window someone had written 'Good Morning'! The ship was a lorry transporter, with ample space for a hundred cars. Sometimes we dig our own pits, and promptly fall into them.

Meanwhile in Athens the politicians, released from internal exile in remote villages, military prisons, and even mental asylums on forbidden islands, were gathering and trying to re-form old parties or to start new ones. The people in the street however had made the decision for them. Crowds started gathering in Syntagma Square, first hundreds on the Tuesday afternoon, then many thousands on Wednesday, chanting *Kara-man-lis einai o anthropos!* over and over again outside the parliament building. An acting president invited him to return from exile in Paris, which he did on the Wednesday afternoon to be sworn in as Prime Minister. Greece appeared happily to think that its problems were over, and the loss of the problematic island of Cyprus would be compensated by the restoration of democratic government at home. Turkey however had other ideas. Thousands were killed on both sides, and Turkey eventually seized almost half of Cyprus.

The Kyklades finally returned to Paros on Thursday. This time we were packed and waiting ready on the quay: you'd better believe it! As we drove away from Piraeus a man on the pavement gestured furiously at me, shouting and waving his fist. I was puzzled; then I realised I was wearing a trophy from my recent trip to Israel – it was a leather desert hat, but from the side it looked quite like a cowboy hat. For reasons I still find hard to understand, many Athenians held the USA and Britain largely responsible for the whole debacle. It seemed for a few weeks as if we had jumped out of the frying pan into the fire by returning to Athens.

Postscript.

It was a beautiful autumn day in Aghia Paraskevi; but there was something else in the air besides the resinous perfume of the skinias pines, which wafted over the gardens and the pavements. Hardly a car moved, all the people walked where they were going with a calm dignity; and the day seemed to be invested with an aura, almost a sort of secular holiness. For the Athenians, usually hurried and curt like most city people, had stopped work, and were going to the polls for the first free elections in years. The Greek people had got their country back.

Robin Brown
Sauverny, France
January 2012

Threshing wheat, Livadia, 1974.
Courtesy of Robin Brown

FLORENCE'S STORY · 1966
By Florence Tamburro

Florence on Paros

After living in Rome for over a year it became obvious that we had to disappear during the summer. Why? It seemed that everyone we knew came to Rome for their holidays to stay at "Pensione O'Grady". Desmond had no quiet time to write. The boys were bored with the city heat, as was I. Consequently, we sublet our flat to a German professor and his family while he was on sabbatical. And we decided to go to Greece.

Our destination was to be the island of Patmos. However, on the Ferry Boat from Brindisi in Italy to Patras in Greece we met a Greek student who was studying at a university in Italy, now on his way back to Greece for the summer. He advised us to go to Paros. His Yaya (grandmother) lived there and he was full of enthusiasm as he described the beaches, which he knew our young sons would love, the characteristic villages, the fresh fish, the friendly welcoming people. Why not? If it wasn't what we expected we could move on.

We stayed in Athens for a few days, enjoying the Parthenon and museums before taking a ferry boat to Paros. The "Ellie" turned out to be a very old ferry with few amenities. However, most of the people aboard were native Parians. We had a marvelous time listening to the young people singing and playing music, as well as dancing the dances of their country. Some of those we met on that first voyage are still close friends of ours.

The port town, Paroikia, although very beautiful, was not exactly what I, at least, was hoping for. However, we were saved by a bus the next morning. I asked a policeman standing at the harbor where that bus was going. "To a small fishing village called Naoussa". We hopped on immediately. It was 1966 and the road between Paroikia and

Naoussa was still a very bumpy dirt road. We wondered if it had been a good idea after all to jump on the bus. After much jerking and coughing the bus managed to reach the top of a steep hill. We saw Paradise before our eyes – the Bay of Naoussa, with a small island between the village and the beaches across the bay, the only structure on it a tiny church. The sea was, and still is, purple/blue/and/or emerald green, and when you stand in it, you can still see your feet as well as the clear, clean sand on the sea floor.

We arrived in this most charming village of Naoussa. As we walked around we knew we would never leave it because no other place could possibly be more beautiful nor be so welcoming.

Then we came upon a unique little harbor. We sat at the kafenion drinking coffee and watching the fishermen unloading their catch off the boats, or mending their nets. A man approached us who spoke some English, which he learned while he was a seaman. "Would you like to have lunch?" He could buy fish from one of the boats which had returned with the catch, and he would cook in his garden taverna. Of course, we were starving by then, and were happy to learn that there was at least one taverna in the village. We accepted, rounded up the boys, and walked with him to his charming garden taverna.

As he served the meal he asked us if we had found a place to stay. We told him we wanted to rent a flat for the summer. He suggested that after we finish our meal, and the siesta hours were over, he would take us around. We had assumed it would be difficult to know where to start in a village with literally no tourism, but we were fortunate to have met this kind man.

We walked through the village with him and his young wife looking at houses here and there, which were for rent. Nothing appealed until we came close to the end of the small village. There was the perfect flat just large enough for a couple with two children. The Tsounaki family, who owned it, lived in a flat, which was attached to ours. Sophia was about my age and had two daughters and two sons. We had a perfect view of the sea all the way to the other side of the bay. Also visible were the remains of an old Venetian fortress at the entrance of the little harbor.

We settled into Sophia's wonderful little house. The next morning we went with the children down to the kafenion on the harbor for our breakfast. Way back then Nescafe was the only choice of coffee, but one can get used to anything. As we sat sipping we noticed a young man high up on a kaiki painting the mast.

He came down and approached us. We asked him to sit down, have a coffee or ouzo. He also knew some English which he learned while he was working on the sea. He, in turn, asked us if we would like to go fishing with him during the siesta hour. We were very excited at the prospect. We met Sergio at 2 pm. He had made a bait line with bits of food attached every few feet. When we were well out into the sea he started dropping the line. Then he sailed to a wee island which wasn't much more than a few large rocks. We all disembarked and went for a swim. However, Sergio donned a pair of flippers, a mask, and carried a spear gun into the sea where he shot and brought back fish for all of us. He then lit a fire, cooked the fish, and we all feasted. On the way back to the harbor he started to pull up the line he had dropped on our way to the island. Every piece of bait had some kind of fish hanging from it, including octopi. Sergio was very fast at pulling them up on deck. The fish were very active, flopping about. However, most exciting was the way he killed the octopus, which was trying to wind his tentacles around

Sergio's arms. He turned the head of the octopus inside out and bit it between the eyes – very fast, no blood – rendered helpless.

As we approached the harbor we espied Sergio's father standing at the entrance threatening with his fist. Was Sergio mad taking tourists out when the wind was starting up?
We were told to meet at the ouzeria at 8 pm for drinks and grilled octopus. There we found many locals whom we had not met yet. Sergio introduced us around: we ate wonderful bits of tender octopus and drank ouzo with joy. That was my introduction to octopus, and I still consider it a delicacy I can't live without. From the ouzeria everyone went to the garden restaurant. By now it was past 10:00 p.m. There were more people we hadn't met, young and old. Our dinner that night was the catch of the day, all the wonderful fresh fish that Sergio brought back with him. Everyone ate and drank with gusto. Those who knew English interpreted what we said for those who didn't know English.

At approximately 11:30 p.m. everyone began to get up out of their chairs. In the middle of the garden was a threshing floor, which was used as the dance floor, probably left there from when there was once a farm. They came to us and asked us to dance with them.

Neither one of us knew how to do Greek dances. The answer to that was, "Don't worry, we will teach you". And teach us they did. Well, I never stopped dancing, sometimes until three or four in the morning for ten years at least. We still do Greek dances at birthdays and other celebrations. It wasn't long before we were invited to join a group of people from the village to travel by bus around the island, stopping at various points of interest. We were thrilled at the prospect since we had no means of transportation to visit the rest of the island. The first stop was Aliki, where we had refreshments as we enjoyed the view of the sea and the multi-colored fishing boats. Then on to Drios for a swim and to lunch just above the beach, with lovely trees for shade and a view of the perfect sea. We lazed about for quite a while before we left for Piso Livadi, which is a very special little village on the sea. It has many interesting restaurants where one can eat raw or cooked seafood in the shell, bright colored fishing boats, and, of course, a beach.

After several more stops we went to Lefkes, which is the highest town on the island. Most of the population had moved from there, but it was one of the popular villages to visit. There were several good tavernas, where, of course, everyone danced after a good dinner and lots of wine. We arrived back in Naoussa very late, but happy with a strong sense of the island and the people who live on it. On the other side of the bay from Naoussa is a series of beaches separated by large rocks which look like pieces of sculpture. The easiest way to get there was by a little boat that went back and forth from the village harbor.

There is no end to the wonderful characters who made up the village. Two brothers ran a kafenion, where we often had breakfast – Giorgo, who was married, therefore left the café around 11p.m.; and Christos stayed on to serve the late comers. He had quite a sense of humor and enjoyed playing tricks on us. When he heard us returning from an evening of eating and dancing, he would close up the cafe. We all knew he was in there, and sure enough, eventually an arm would come through the window with a bottle of wine in it. It would be left on the table followed by some glasses. One night the window opened, but there was no bottle of wine. Instead we saw a hose aimed at us. We all became very wet and joined him in a hearty laugh.

Then there was Captain Leonardis, who captained a beautiful large kaiki, the very one we saw Giorgos painting the first day we arrived in Naoussa. He brought food and other goods from island to island. The Captain, as he was called, was a very strong character, who had a limp and never wore shoes unless he was leaving the island. A common scene as he was about to leave was his wife, Aspasia, running after him with his shoes in her hand.

The day we were to leave the island in order to return to Rome, we were talking with The Captain who asked us if we would like to go as far as Syros on his kaiki. Of course, we were thrilled. It didn't matter to us that the other passengers on board were cows. And so, off we went, the five of us, Desmond, myself, and the three boys, Bryan, Mahlon, and Leonardo. Bryan, my eldest son, was at that time imitating Douglas Fairbanks Jr., rushing around the boat as though he were a pirate, even though we were entering an area of rough sea. Poor Mahlon became very ill. I was carrying Leonardo, my youngest, then one year old, on my lap. The Captain decided I should be in a safer position. He hoisted me up on top of an oil tank, put little Leonardo on my lap, and tied us to the mast. I felt as though I was in a Metro Golden Mayer epic film when, without warning, Leonardo vomited on the head of Mahlon, who was vomiting over the edge of the kaiki just below. This was where The Captain took over and cleaned him up. Desmond and Bryan were the only members of the family who managed to feel as well when we arrived in Syros as they did before we left Paros. I felt very unstable, my legs were wobbling, my head spinning, the earth swaying from side to side. The Captain took me by the elbow, led me into a cafe, ordered fresh squeezed lemon juice, and told me to drink it down. I obeyed. As soon as I finished drinking it the earth stopped swaying, my head stopped spinning, and my legs held up beneath me.

Well, it is all history, of course, but I still go every year to stay in the charming village, where I now have more friends than anywhere else on earth, both the village people and those who come every year from different parts of the world.

Florence Tamburro,
Cambridge,
 Ma. USA.
March 2012

Desmond O'Grady
Courtesy of Florence Tamburro

PHILLADA'S STORY · 1968
By Phillada Lecomte

Phillada ca. 1968

There is no real **beginning** to this story as I believe all things are interconnected. Maybe we need to go back to the historic night of April 6th, 1941, when the German bombardment of Piraeus harbour began.

Two Australian Naval officers returning hastily, under the wailing sirens, to their ship H.M.A.S. Perth, moored in the bay of Piraeus, discovered the ammunition ship "Clan Fraser" burning fiercely after a direct hit. Alongside lay a large barge full of explosives. They realized that if the ship were to blow up, it would ignite the lighter and the whole port could be blown to pieces. They heroically rowed across in a simple skiff and managed to detach the laden ammunition barge, towing it away from the burning ship. Suddenly an immense explosion ripped through the "Clan Fraser" and flying wreckage and falling metal and debris filled the sky. A surging tidal wave sucked the two men deep down into the dirty, oily waters, but luckily the 4,000 tons of explosives had sunk and the men's efforts had probably saved thousands of lives. They were found on the surface, dazed but alive, covered in oil, by a passing Greek trawler and taken to the Greek Naval Hospital, whose beds were full of shattered glass from the explosion. They were dressed in long, white nightshirts, treated for shock with plenty of Metaxa brandy! and were later found and returned safely to their worried Captain aboard the H.M.A.S Perth. For that heroic action, my father, Commander Warwick Bracegirdle (Gunnery Officer R.AN), was awarded the high honour of Distinguished Service Cross (D.S.C.), and his deep connection with the people of Greece would bring us all later to the island of Paros.

The Greek poet **Odysseus Elytis** wrote, "Greece, I have reached this conclusion now for a long time, is a concentration of senses. To be Greek means to feel and to react in a certain way - nothing more. It is a realm of being that has a direct relation with the drama of Darkness and of Light that all of us are enacting out here in this corner of the globe". The Cyclades are islands of Light, a circle of rocky islands in the windswept Aegean Sea, dancing around the sacred isle of Delos, where the Sun God Apollo was born. This mystery of light (Fos) and breath (Pnevma) immersed itself into every one of these ancient islands and the spirit of their people.

After my father's devotion to duty in World War 2 and his ship's assistance in the evacuation of foreign troops in the Battle of Crete in 1941, his link with the Greek people was strong. After a life of duty and family in Australia and England, when he retired and was separated from my mother, he returned to Greece in 1965. His wish was to co-operate with local captains to sail around the islands with tourists. A friendly, charming man, wearing his famous beret, he was warmly welcomed by the locals in Naoussa and with little Greek he quickly won the fishermen's hearts through the language of ouzo and suma!! His little sailing skiff "Gitana" took him across the Naoussa bay to Kolimbithres. Above the volcanic sculpted rocks he rented a primitive cottage. The fishing port of Naoussa, on the north coast of Paros, had a Lilliputian, Byzantine port with a fishermen and farmer community and at that time very few foreign visitors. Its narrow, labyrinth streets, painted paving stones and its white cubical houses, had hardly changed since Venetian times, when it had been a pirates' haven. The miniature port, full of colourful," caique" fishing boats, was made of great slabs of ancient Parian marble, strewn with maroon and orange fishing nets. Here the well-known, mustached Captain Linardos befriended the Aussie Commander" Warwick", as he came to be called, and a strong friendship of sharing the seas on his beautiful two- masted caique began. Captain Linardos, always at the port barefoot, struck a piratical figure with his splendid mustache and tame seagull perched on his shoulder. Across the bay, where the Russian fleet of Catherine the Great had moored in the 1770s, on the rocks by the sea, stood the ruins of the Monastery of St John, Agios Ioannis o Detis. Here had arrived in 1965, the Dutch painter Gisele d'Ailly, and her husband, the former Mayor of Amsterdam, Arnold d'Ailly. They had discovered this idyllic, ruined setting far away from anywhere, and obtained permission from the monks at Longovarda Monastery to restore it and rebuild the chapel, then inhabited only by goats. So began a special friendship between the eccentric Aussie Commander and the adventurous Dutch artistic couple.

In the summer of 1968, with the student uprising in Paris, the wave of change and the influence of the swinging Sixties had generated a new sense of freedom, which encouraged many people, artists, writers and adventure seekers, to search for new meanings in their lives. However, in Greece the Colonels, on 21st April 1967, had staged a very unpopular military coup. The climate of dictatorship was not favourable to many liberals; martial law was imposed. During the Junta, many thousands of Greeks were tortured, sent to prison and into forced exile. In spite of this, an adventurous couple, a young, blonde-haired girl Phillada (myself) and her bearded, longhaired partner Gerard, a French artist, set off in summer with their backpacks, hitch-hiking from France on their journey of self-discovery, to meet her father, the Commander, on Paros.

In 1968, to get to Paros by boat was long and often rough, so after six hours or so, the old ferry boat "Elli" arrived under darkness in the bay of Paroikia. We were taken ashore by a small dinghy and brought to the quay on a black, starry night. Stumbling our way out of the port, we lay down exhausted under the stars, on a rare patch of soft grass and fell asleep, with an intoxicating smell of jasmine. We awoke suddenly to bright light with cascading water drenching us and the face of the curious gardener, peering at us in the morning sun. Kalimera and welcome to Paros!! We had slept in the municipal park right opposite the old Post Office. Some Greek coffees and koulouria later, we were soon rattling along by bus over the dusty hills to Naoussa, down past the green vineyards of Kamares to the gleaming, sapphire waters of the bay of Naoussa. The small, white, houses, like glistening, sugar lumps nestled behind a hill beckoning. We were warmly welcomed, but with no phones and a slow postal system my father had not known of our arrival, so he had left the island. Everyone in the village offered us hospitality, but the old couple who owned my father's house, Papou and Yaya Tsounakis, proposed that we should stay at another house across the bay. In 1968 there was still intensive farming activity all over the island. Our journey in the back of an old truck was memorable. The countryside was covered in swaying, golden terraces of wheat and barley, like a vivid Van Gogh painting, scattered with dancing, scarlet poppies and bright yellow marguerites. What smells!! What sounds!! What light!! We were enchanted. The tiny, solitary house on the rocky hillside was made of stone and whitewashed from local marble limestone, with a shady terrace of grapevines and jasmine. There was no kitchen, no bathroom, nor running water, nor electricity; just two small cool rooms, tiny windows looking out to sea, earthen floors, a platform bed, paraffin lamps, a flat clay roof and a deep cool well and marble trough to wash in. Everywhere the eye could see were warm rocky walls, rustling wheat, goats and donkeys grazing and the vast bowl of the dancing sea below. Opposite lay the speckled white houses of Naoussa and far away the misty, marble mountains of Naxos. We had arrived in Paradise!!

Born in the southern hemisphere in Sydney, Australia, I was later brought up in the grey, wet climes of England and studied French language and literature in France, but had always longed for this spiritual reconnection with nature, warmth and wilderness. For Gerard, an artist from the south of France, Paros was somehow reminiscent of Provence, an opportunity for intense creativity, where he began his journey into marble carving and drawing.

It was on Paros that we discovered the peace and freedom of a simple life amongst warm-hearted, generous people; a destiny in life that would bring me a real sense of belonging and a joyful connection with the earth, sea and these island people.

Below in the distance was the blue dome of the Monastery of St John, which Gisele d'Ailly had lovingly restored, where she came every summer to paint. She had led an extraordinary life, endangering herself in the war, selflessly helping Jewish poets to hide from the Nazis. She was full of enthusiasm and childlike curiosity for life. We soon became very good friends, often joining her for meals and poetry readings with the many interesting poets and artists that would come to stay with her. Later she was to commission Gerard to sculpt marble for the chapel. Except for Gisele, the only house nearby us was the working farmhouse below, surrounded by threshing floors, dovecotes, stables, wells and fields of grapevines. Here lived and toiled a large, Parian family, Georgios and Marousso Zoumis, with their six children, two girls and four boys. They kept more than two hundred goats and sheep, horses, mules, donkeys, geese, turkeys, doves, dogs, cats and chickens; so many mouths to feed.

Theirs was a very hard life. Parian farmers at the time were very much self-sufficient, consuming mainly only the products of their land. They would ride their mules to Naoussa to exchange goat's cheese, goat's meat or olive oil, for sugar, coffee, rice and paraffin for light. Almost everything else they needed they grew themselves. My partner Gerard and I were adopted by this welcoming family into their home and hearts. Marousso became like a second mother to me, a deep connection was formed that continues to this day. She was a powerful icon of fortitude for her large family. A great honour, many years later was to hear the old man Georgios say,"I have three daughters, two of my own and you Phillada!" Their day began long before sunrise, milking two hundred goats and sheep is no easy task. Lifting up heavy buckets of water by rope from the deep well was hard work. The younger son would sleepily be put on his donkey to trot off far away to primary school in Kamares, while the other sons and daughters were all at home helping their parents until they married. From our house, the mountains at dawn, blushing violet in the early morning softness, before the harsh light and heat of day, would echo out with the melodic harmony of goat bells, cascading down from the rocks, and the yearning donkey's cry.

Each time of year had its special burden of work. The Colonels had cancelled all the farmers' debts to get them on their side, so, although the dictatorship was very unpopular, many of the farmers were prospering. In the summer heat came the wheat harvest, reaped by hand with sickles. In the 70s as tractors began to appear they were very envied, as harvesting under the relentless sun was a backbreaking task. The sheaves were taken to the round, stone threshing floors (the aloni) found all over the Cycladic landscape. Here, the poor, muzzled mules, tied together, would be whipped by the thresher, driven round and around the circle to the lilting call of, " Ley, ley, ley, ley", until their pounding hooves would separate the grain from the chaff. The golden grain would lie in piles on the stones and the straw forked and winnowed into the wind. Those famous swirling winds of the deep blue Aegean, whipping up the white horses, sometimes bringing angry winter storms and rain, and in summer, the cool, refreshing northern Meltemi winds. No wonder the god of winds, Aeolus, was so revered in ancient times. The many windmills of Paros, so typical a sight in the Cyclades, were still stone-grinding wheat, rye and barley grain into the late 70s. When it was baking day, Marouso would holler up the mountain to me, her voice bouncing off the stones, "Ella, come Phillada, It's time for the fire," and I would bound down the rocky path to help her. First, we had to light the fire using the dried, prickly bushes lying out in the yard. Paros has little wood so these wild bushes were collected and dried for firewood. The big stone ovens would become ablaze with red embers, which were wiped away with a wet rag on a long stick when the stones were hot and ready for the plump loaves and earthenware pots, full of delicious bean stew. Everyone baked their own bread to feed their large families. A huge pile of sticky dough in the long wooden trough (skafi) needed strength to be pummelled and kneaded, until it became like a baby's bottom! Then it was rolled in sesame seeds, wrapped in cloth and put to rise under warm blankets. Many superstitions and beliefs from pagan times abound, mixed together with their devout Orthodox faith. Marouso would ask me to place a box of matches on the rising loaves and in her belief the consciousness of the dough would listen and know it was time for the fire. The many wholemeal loaves baked in the stone oven would last a large family a week.

After the 15th August, the feast of the Panayia, (the Holy Mother), celebrated by crowds at the great 6th century Byzantine church of the Ekatontapiliani in Paroikia, would later come the joyous Trigos, the grape harvest. Paros since antiquity has been renowned for its sweet, red wine. No chemicals were used on the land, only manure. After the ripe grapes were picked, they were sometimes laid on the ground to sweeten for some days, then put into baskets called koufinia, loaded onto mules and taken to the patitiri (the treading place). This was newly whitewashed every season. Asvesti, the local whitewash derived from limestone, became obligatory for painting island homes more than three hundred years ago, as leprosy existed then and it was used as a disinfectant. The grapes would be piled up in great clusters, bursting with juice, and we would climb in barefooted, singing, laughing and dancing to squish them down until the must ran deep red, pouring out into the vats below to be taken to the awaiting barrels. Many songs and dances evoke the treading of the grapes since antiquity. The notion that we were linked through these sacred practices to the ancient Greek God of wine, Dionysos (Bacchus), in a long chain of tradition, was a powerful feeling for me. As **Kostas Palamas** a Greek poet wrote, "The soul of Ancient Greece lives on, hidden unwillingly within us. Great Pan is not dead. No, great Pan does not die!!" The barrels were left open for forty days for the wine to ferment, and mountain thyme was placed in the openings to prevent the fruit flies from spoiling the wine, giving it a special aroma. The first grape juice, musto, was boiled into a tasty, sticky sweet, dark dessert made with flour, almonds and cinnamon and covered with sesame seed, known as mustalevria. Forty days is an important, religious, symbolical number respected in the Greek Orthodox faith, originating from the feast of the Ascension, when Christ, after forty days, ascends to heaven. So, forty days of fasting before Christmas and Easter, forty days of confinement for the mother who had just given birth, forty days of mourning before the first remembrance and forty days for the wine to ferment. About forty days after the trigos, when the wine had fermented in the barrels, came the alchemy of distilling the fermented stalks and skins of the pressed grapes for the local "suma" or tsipouro alcohol. This had been outlawed during the Junta years, but was often done at night with the magical sight of shining copper kettles, black cauldrons and blazing fire. Riding at night into the hills on donkeys and tasting the fiery, warm, freshly-distilled liquor was exciting, except if you drank too much you were liable to fall off your donkey on the way home and land in a prickle bush!

Sometime in October, the barren fields with every stalk of straw eaten by the hungry goats, would be strewn with animal manure, hauled out of the stables by mule loads to cover the fields before the first rains. Marouso, with her earth goddess quality, as the matriarch of the family would decide which fields would be sown that year and in an ancient ritual, going right back to Persephone, crushed deep red pomegranate seeds would be thrown over the awaiting earth as a symbol of fertility. When the first rains at last came, after maybe six months of drought, the silver ploughs would be out piercing the wet earth working their way up and down the single furrows, pulled by two obedient, straining mules and the farmer's cry, "Aro arona re wheest" would sound out across the fields. Papou Tsounakis, the old twinkling-eyed farmer, would hire Gerard, my partner, for eighty drachmas a day (then £1=75 drachmas) to help him plough his land. This old man had fought in the First World War campaign of Asia Minor in Turkey on camelback, had survived on dry crusts of bread and was as strong as an ox. He would stop after long hours of work, just for a short break to eat bread, olives and cheese. He was dressed in the usual farmers attire, woollen hand-woven trousers, fanela, a hand knitted sweater and the woollen cummerbund (zonari) that all farmers wore winter and summer, a long knitted band to protect their backs from damp and strain. Gerard and I would also work along with the farmers for our keep to help cut the cane (kalami) used for all the roofs in the islands. This was difficult work, filling our hands with nasty splinters. These canes were used woven together on top of the beams, then came a layer of insulating, dried seaweed. Each year the dry clay, volcanic earth from Santorini known as "porcelani" would be laid on the roof tops which, when swollen with the first rains, would become waterproof.

After the ploughing season, in November came the precious harvest for the sacred oil. We would ride on donkeys up over the hills, past the beautiful dome of the 17th century Agios Andreas Monastery to the fertile valley of Marathi, renowned for the ancient quarries, from where came the famous "Lichnites" translucent, Parian marble. The arduous, backbreaking task came of first picking up, one by one, the many fallen olives off the ground, before laying out the sheets (no fancy nets in those days) under the trees. The beautiful, tall, knarled olive trees in Marathi and Lefkes in the centre of the island can be as old as five hundred years. After a long, cold day's work, it was a satisfying sight to see the bursting sacks and baskets of ripe olives laden on the donkeys' backs. The dancing, silver, olive trees in golden, winter sunlight, the singing women and the laughter and gossip that went on while they worked was a friendly sight. The ground would be covered in horta, the many kinds of wild, bitter, winter greens that are a delicious diet in winter, picked by the women after the rains. The abundance of the earth in winter was plentiful: snails, wild mushrooms, wild asparagus, volvi, the bulb of a flower and the delicate purple crocuses, whose yellow saffron stamens coloured the local suma drink. For many weeks, even months, the daily task of olive- picking, still carried on today by members of the family, was an important part of their lives to obtain this precious oil. Around six kilos of olives is needed to produce just one litre of stone- pressed pure oil, and as well as for the home, oil was always offered to the church or chapels to keep the very important icon lamps burning all year. The first pink cyclamens and candle- like asphodels would appear miraculously out of the dry earth in autumn, and later in early spring after the winter rains, came the delicate almond blossom and an amazing array of wild flowers. Out of the barren earth came a rainbow of colours, blue and purple irises, lupins, grape hyacinths, myriad colours of anemones, miniature pink gladioli, scented baby narcissi and the rare, dwarf bee orchids, often only to be found in the Cyclades. Later, the hills would be full of the aroma of flowering oregano, sage and thyme, essential for teas and cooking.

As well as their hard, daily life, the Parian people respected the many religious saints' days with their powerful devotion to their Orthodox faith. Pasca, Eastertime, was always the great celebration of the year, when, after candlelit midnight mass, the village echoed with Christos Anesti!! Alithos Anesti! Truly he has risen. Easter Sunday became a day of feasting, after the long fast, with red dyed eggs, roasted lambs on the spit, wild music and dancing in traditional costumes. Before Easter, on Clean Monday, everyone would set off for the sea and picnic with Lenten food, octopus, kalamari and shellfish on the rocks. Octopus would be caught and in that age-old practice be thrown, dashed onto the rocks, multiple times, they say a hundred! to soften the tentacles. On people's name days, yiorti, we would be often invited to go along, even in winter by moonlight, rain or in fierce winds. Arriving in the dark stables by donkey, the women would change into their good clothes next to the steaming animals, giggling and emerging into the bright gaslight to live music and gaiety. This was how the young girls met a future husband so everyone was eyeing each other. Some young girls shone out with their shy, innocent, bashful beauty, lowering their dark eyes when spoken to. In the 70s the custom was still for the men to sit at a laden table to drink and eat, and the poor women had to serve or sit stiffly, sipping little glasses of very sweet liqueur and eating sticky cakes. Being the only foreigners there, and seeing Gerard tucking in to all this feast, I caused much laughter when I decided it was time the women had some fun too, so amidst my feminist protests, having stirred up the macho hierarchy, reluctantly they allowed us to join in also and clink glasses crying," Viva, Viva" "Yamas", health to us, wishing, "Chronia Polla", many years, and to partake of all the delicious homemade food. Spinach and cheese pies, stuffed grape leaves, tiny fried fish, steaming plates of roasted goat's meat, fragrant, fresh, green, olive oil, myzithra, fresh sheep's cheese, and the farmer's own red wine flowed in abundance. At many festivals there were local musicians, often the old shepherd Barber Yannis, a great zabouna bagpipe player, who made beautiful goatskin bagpipes, with delicately sculpted cane flutes. The music and singing was very lively and stirring, the bagpipes gave the drone accompanied by a clarino, violi, a type of violin and tambour. The local favourite island dance, the Ballos, from the Italian" ballare" to dance, was made popular during the Venetian occupation. This is a subtle flowing in and out of the partners, barely touching each other but flirtatious, then drifting away. Then there is the ancient chain dance, the Syrtos, performed gracefully. The circle dances like Kalamatiano were danced with women holding a handkerchief between their hands, swaying in and out in repetitive steps round and round like the flowing sea. Sacred circle dances from ancient times. I love dancing and dancing with them seemed to be a great way to be accepted as I could join in and mingle. Some of the old farmers were the best dancers, even with their sturdy boots they could leap and their feet barely touched the ground. The young, shy men needed lots more wine before they would enter the dance floor. Music and dance have always been an important part of these islanders' lives. Music for the Ancient Greeks was a supreme art aimed at harmonising body and mind. Sometimes we witnessed lively farmers' weddings, where wild music, dancing and moving "mirologia" songs, spontaneously sung from the soul, would keep us up all night, when emerging into the moonlight we would be sleepily taken home by our faithful donkeys. **Desmond O'Grady**, the wild Irish poet known by many, lived also in the 70s in Naoussa. He wrote of the peoples' need for the dance". Some fine poems of his written on the island speak deeply of the people of Paros and their joys and sufferings. During those years, with her Rolleiflex camera, my dear friend Stella Lubsen was able to document many of these amazing moments and since then has had exhibitions on Paros, where the rich cultural heritage that we were so privileged to share, has been beautifully preserved. There was a meeting of hearts, in those days of few visitors, between those rather eccentric, bohemian foreigners and the simple, pure people of Paros. Their strong sense of filoxenia, hospitality, gave us all this warmth and sense of having arrived home where we belonged.

Apart from our integration in those first early years with the local farmers and Naoussa, because of lack of transport, we had little contact with foreigners on the other side of the island. I used to go shopping in Naoussa riding on a donkey, trotting round the bay and once was reprimanded by the local policeman because my donkey had sullied the paving stones. I hadn't put a bag under his tail!! Great progress came when the poor donkey carried our first petrolgas bottle home to cook with, instead of the laborious task of cooking with wood. These gas bottles were carried on the decks of the caiques from Piraeus and were very sought after. I learnt quickly to speak Greek, albeit with an island accent and mistakes, but languages and poetry had always been my passion and I studied Greek poetry, while at home we would speak together in French. We had the BBC World Service on a tiny radio which kept us linked to the outside world and a primitive battery record player, where I would play my nostalgic Joan Baez, Beatles and Bob Dylan records. There were few cars, or motorbikes so about once a week we set off on foot to the main road to get a bus to Paroikia town, where we delighted in a rare cake treat from the zacharoplasteio, could pick up our mail and buy supplies in the Agora. One of the small bachaliko grocery stores, where you could buy everything from nails and paraffin to tarama and tasty farmer's cheese, can still be found in the market today, kept proudly by dear Kostas, O "Mourlas", still full of barrels and lamps. As we had no electricity, we kept all our perishables in a basket deep down our well, fresh even in summer. I tried to grow a garden watered by our well, but alas the goats thought it was delicious and I came home one day to devastation. We rarely ate meat and got most of our supplies from the farmers. Everyone in town was kind and friendly and the produce was fresh and local. Parians, many with loans, slowly began to build hotels and some began to sell off their land. We made friends with the burgeoning artist community who began to live here. The now well-reputed American Aegean Center for the fine arts had begun to attract young students to the island, Gerard began to carve blocks of marble and I began my interest in weaving. At that time, more tourists and foreigners began to arrive, some came to live in the countryside, renting and buying up old homes and enjoying this simple life. Many of them, writers and artists, would meet for animated discussions at the local cafes, sharing their hopes and ideas, learning from each other.

Through our close friendship with Gisele d'Ailly, we had befriended Stella and Koos Lubsen, who visited in summer from those early years. We would delight in sharing the discovery and freedom of this extraordinary land, milking the goats, dancing under the moonlight, swimming and exploring the rocky sea caves and mountain tops, and learning all the local traditions; they were very happy times. The lighthouse keeper, Kostas Vionis, came in his free time to help Gisele whitewash every year the huge walls of the monastery of St John. He was a cheerful, friendly man, a keen beekeeper, eager to share with us all the knowledge of the local traditions. He manned the lighthouse at the northern rocky point of the island and kept his fishing dinghy in the bay, returning to his wife and children in town every few days. He has remained a firm friend to this day and is still one of Paros's fine beekeepers. We met also a unique, gentle, older Greek friend, a true wise philosopher, poet and painter called Stelios Prassinos, who had taught himself many languages. In his 80s, a solitary man, he was happy for intellectual company, and walked every day through Kamares valley to Naoussa and often visited us. Until his death he continued to document and paint the local landscapes with delicate precision. It would be impossible to not include my friendship with the magical dancer Vassili Yacoumis, loved by so many; his unique, artistic expression of spontaneity and freedom warmed so many hearts. Gisele d'Ailly had been extremely kind and generous, and apart from restoring the entire monastery, she had helped many poor people in Naoussa, especially a fisherman who had twelve children. She helped Dimitri buy his caique to go out and fish for his family and in return every Sunday, early in the rose-coloured morning he would proudly chug over the bay to the rocks of Agios Ioannis to take Gisele to church and do her weekly shopping. Later, after 1975, when we went to live with Gisele to help her at the monastery, this was the big excitement of the week, going to the village with the caique for shopping, chatting with our local friends of Naoussa and eating some tasty food at a taverna. Gisele d'Ailly has led a fascinating and rich artistic life and will be an amazing one hundred years old this year!

In the early 70s, I befriended an extraordinary local Greek Orthodox nun, called Antonia. She lived alone opposite Isterni in her monastery of Agios Antonios, which she had built herself with pick and shovel out of nothing. Sister Antonia, born in Brooklyn, U.S.A was the child of Greek-Americans and as a young woman had several visions of St Anthony, who urged her to go back to her native Greece and build a monastery. Inspired, she came to Paros and on the hill above Naoussa began to dig out the rocky ground and with help from some devout locals, she built a primitive house and took orders as a nun in the Orthodox faith as a Paleomerologitissa (order of the Old Calendar). Until 1923, the Orthodox Church followed the old Julian calendar, which was thirteen days ahead of the present Gregorian calendar. Devout and strong, with many talents and faith, she slowly built her chapel and monastery. In the early years, she wove woollen cloth on a huge loom for men's suits and as a brilliant craftswoman, managed to support herself and help orphans and the poor. This meeting was an important stage of my life on Paros. Antonia introduced me to this beast of wood and steel and taught me how to weave; many of the convents on Paros had looms and this was an island tradition. I wrote at the time to express my emotion about her. "A studio with beams of olive, skins of whitewash, a carpet of well-swept earth, for my joy a beast of wood and steel, which sings and dances beneath my feet, for friend a nun, robed in black, a black yellowed by so much sun, her face pure devotion, smile releasing her goodness within, the new moon came to light the threads like an outstretched harp on my loom. Lavender my hands, rose my feet, until the darkness fell. The shuttle has sung, incense smokes in the rocky cave and the holy oil lights up our sacred dreams". Her two brothers, devout monks of Mount Athos, would visit her and I had the great honour to join them in liturgy. As the sun rose up over Naxos, the first golden rays lit up the dark shapes of the bearded, praying monks, blessing us with intoxicating incense and the small chapel decorated with precious icons was filled with their pure Byzantine chanting""Kyrie Eleison". Thus began an intense friendship with the nun and a journey into carding wool, spinning, dyeing, washing the sheep in the sea at Agios Ioannis and weaving tapestries. Every year in summer, painstakingly the sheep would be shorn by hand with clippers, then the flock would be driven by the sea. Georgios and his strong sons would lift the bleating, protesting sheep into the sea to be dunked under to cleanse their pink naked bodies of any lice or ticks. In wintertime we would sit in the farmhouse sorting and carding the oily wool, which Marouso would skillfully teeze, twist and spin on her "roka", the weighted spindle which was used as far back as Minoan times. As I learnt these new skills, our tiny house filled with raw wool and I began to weave rag rugs and natural woollen wall tapestries with organic forms. Most women at that time had looms in their homes to weave the traditional rag rugs, made by cutting up old, coloured strips of clothes and beating them into rugs for the cold stone floors. Nothing would go to waste. Gerard would paint and draw skillfully long into the night by the light of the paraffin lamp, something similar to Picasso's famous" Blue Period" painted by the light of candles, while I carded and spun the wool. We had minimal funds but were young, strong and happy and lived very simply and economically; no bills, nor telephone, nor travel. Some winters were bitterly cold, buffeted by the strong, north, gale-force winds, the pelting rain keeping us indoors for days, fixing the leaks in our earthen roof with buckets under the drips. Some winter nights, in spite of their hard day's work and fatigue the family would invite us and they would still have enough energy and kefi to jump up and dance the night away. One summer, in order to survive, having been stopped selling paintings in the Plaka by the Junta secret police, we left for Italy to sell paintings at the picturesque tourist port of Positano, near Naples. There the Italians were very generous and bought many of Gerard's paintings, landscapes quickly painted in the street. We did so well we were able to return and live for a year or more on our earnings. It was life lived in the moment.

Then in 1973, a special event occurred which brought us all a happy life change, our baby daughter Gaea, the Earth goddess, was born. She was born at my father's house in England, because by then the Commander had left Paros and with his second wife, Polly, whom he had met on Paros in 1965, had returned to live in England. So everything **is** interconnected! After that our winters were spent in Paris where Gerard and his twin brother ran an engraving press for artists. While her father worked in his studio, I would push my baby around the great corridors of the Louvre museum, keeping warm and inspiring ourselves!! Back on Paros in the summers we went to stay by

Gisele's monastery, while Gerard sculpted marble and little Gaea learnt to scramble up rocks, her days spent learning how to swim and playing with baby lambs, goats and cats. My mother Eve, a great lover of Greece, now ninety-seven, visited us then and delighted in the landscape and sea and her grandchild. It was on Paros that she also wrote some fine poems evoking the beauty and mystery of the island. I quote her in prose: "You ask me why? Why the questioning mind needs the stark solitude of a barren hill, stones sharp beneath the feet, a burning blue sky dome filled with a rushing wind, leaping from the north, tossing olives and tamarisks and cresting the dark sapphire surge. This need to find a meaning, to find this answer may take half a life- a life, what is it anyway? Touch the warm marble and you may feel a million years of being on your palm. Rise up at dawn and swim out into the pathway of the rising sun and cradled on the warm Aegean wave gaze down into the calm, translucent depths. There you can see the bare bones of it all. The "why" the "wherefore" but, not yet the "when".

This period was rich with creativity and friendship with Gisele and the farmers and was a marvellous haven for a child. Somehow, before that there was curiosity from the locals as we were not married and had no child, but as soon as Gaea was born it seemed suddenly we were totally accepted as having fulfilled our duty and a child was an open invitation to everyone's hearts Everytime Marouso baked bread she would always bake a small one for her. The Greeks worship children and when they are small spoil them no end. Little smiling Gaea was already chatty in three languages, learning Greek fast, she spoke with me in English, and with her father in French.

On the 23rd July 1974, when the Junta finally fell, Greece rejoiced and returned to democracy. Exiled artists, musicians and writers returned to create and work in Greece, wonderful music was heard again. It was, however, a bitter sweet time for Greeks and Cypriots, because at the time the Colonels fell, three days before, on the 20th July 1974, Turkey invaded Cyprus and thousands of Cypriot refugees were forced to flee their homeland. Life in Greece came under immense change. More foreigners came to Paros to buy houses and land, the locals prospered and loans were given to assist the tourist development. Electricity began to come to the countryside; poles marched across the land that before had been unmarred for centuries. We moved away to a house up the rocky mountain, where I continued to weave and then in 1977, when Gaea was four, we went to live in the valley of Kamares, an easier place to be with a small child, where later she went to the small primary school with twelve other children. As the only foreign child she was very popular and on her way home on foot through the fields she was often fed by all the grannies she charmed. My Irish friend Fionnuala and I bought pedal motorbikes that gave us a newfound freedom to be able to visit friends with our children without the long hour's walk to town. Many foreigners had small children too, so we would meet so that the children could play together. Later, when we moved to live on Lesvos, my daughter finished Greek primary school with distinction before continuing in France, Britain and Italy. A colourful, multilingual education indeed!

Many wonderful images and memories abound of that magical time more than forty years ago. I feel we related well to the hospitable local Parians, perhaps because of our rather modest means we struggled and led simple lives and were accepted into their hearts, especially because we worked with them and could speak with them and exchange ideas, joys and hardships together.

I have seen many of them as small children grow up to prosper and now have children of their own, sharing weddings, baptisms and funerals together, so whole generations have passed through my life without me realizing how time has flown. I also became a grandmother, with two lively grandsons in Italy. Perhaps also because I am still leading a simple isolated life, I have kept my strong contact with these people. After leaving the island in the early 1980s to move to Lesvos, life took me to London, and for many years I led walking holidays in the wild, rocky mountains of the Mani, Peloponnese..

My journeys took me to India, where I taught English to Tibetan refugees and pursued my growing interest in Buddhism. This strangely brought me back to Paros, which beckoned again in 2002, when I lived for some time in the peaceful sanctuary of the former Buddhist Centre in the Butterfly Valley. Since then, I return to Paros each year and, in the last six years have been happy to offer my unique experience of traditional life here to enrich visitors in their discovery of these ancient islands. When someone asks me where I come from I answer, "I was born Australian but my heart is Greek".

As you have read, this was not really **my** story, it is the story of the people of Paros, and like its beginning it certainly does not have a recognizable end. I did not name many of the wonderful friends whom I met at that time, and who are still here, foreign and Greek, but they are certainly not forgotten. This story speaks of a personal, continuous spiritual involvement with the heart and "pathos" of this ancient land and its people. It is dedicated to those men and women whose joys, songs and laments are reflected with Light and Darkness into their faces and hands. The struggle of their lives shines out from their gaze and in spite of vanishing traditions in a rapidly changing world, the visions and memories of this ancient translucent land will never fade. As the triumphant song taken from **Yannis Ritsos's** Romiosini poem goes," This earth is theirs and ours, and no-one can ever take it from us!" Always when I pass by the bejeweled port of Naoussa, I can still imagine the" Commander" sitting at the kafeneion with his black beret, smiling with his twinkling eyes, raising his glass to us all. Yamas!!! Viva.

The beginning of a circle is also its end.
Heraclitus - 540 BC

Phillada Lecomte, Paros, Greece, May, 2012.

Phillada bathing daughter Gaea, 1974.
Courtesy of Phillada Lecomte

DEIRDRE'S STORY · 1969
By Deirdre Grieve

Deidre with husband Mike and sons
Christopher and Lucien

'So, you were . . . a hippy?' That's the stock response when I tell someone I've been coming to Paros since 1969. Well, no. We came to Paros on a package. An early, aberrant and loosely put together package of four (my third son's arrival still four years off) but a package nonetheless, £79 for a fortnight's flight-inclusive full board at the Naoussa Hotel.

On that August day in '69 we stepped off the ferryboat Elli in our zeitgeist-defying drip-dry holiday clothes onto an unfrequented quayside where a solitary taxi was waiting. For us. So we never did the Ithaka thing, no Laistrygonians or Phoenician trading centres on the way, just a scheduled stop at Syros where loukoumia sellers clambered on board, and before that a taxi in Athens shared with the then Dr. Who, Jon Pertwee, packaged for Mykonos by the same pioneering tour operator and confirming our sense of extra-terrestrial if not divine intervention.

For I *had* done the reading . . . had long since decided that the Cyclades were the closest thing to heaven on earth and had, somewhere, read about Paros, so that, opening this miniscule brochure and finding a picture of the Naoussa Hotel perched on the rocks above Piperi Beach, I made only a token nod to family democracy before I picked up the phone and booked. And booked again and again, adapting to flight-only deals as they were invented, adding a baby, dropping off a teenager to make his own way there, marry, bring children. When my husband died in 1995 we all came to Naoussa to remember him, my eldest son and his wife already expecting their first child. And it was on that trip that I discovered that Naoussa now had an estate agent, and after all the years of talking about it viewed a ruined farmhouse, fell for it, lost it, and ended up with a bijou newly built house now hidden in a sprawling garden where the baby palm trees we planted have grown tall enough to sit under, the olive trees give more oil than we need and my grandchildren all agree that Paros is their favourite place.

The Paros we fell in love with that first year consisted mainly of Naoussa and Kolymbithres. There was little transport and no need to go further. For breakfast on our first morning in what was, I think, the only hotel in Naoussa, Jordanis and Maria Maroulides brought us each a pool of honey on a yellow plate with a basket of still warm bread, then we wandered into the village, saw our first blue dome, first donkey, and, arriving in a state of euphoria at the harbour, where in place of tavernas there were fish stores and instead of tables fishermen mending nets, were approached by a man who asked us if we'd like to go to a beach across the bay. We shook our heads. No swimming things. Half an hour, he said. And so it was that before ten o-clock on our first day we were the only passengers in Yannis Papadakis's caique crossing the bay to share the lovely coves of Kolymbithres with just three or four other families.

 Ours was a full-board deal and there were, anyway, no boats in the afternoon. The siesta hour then was extreme and total as if a spell cast on the village routinely poleaxed the entire population (explaining to this day the logic-defying use of the word 'afternoon': one can only name what one experiences - life after six). So we returned for lunch and found the ouzeria on the harbour edge specially opened for the crew of, I think, the Livanos yacht, ashore for provisions, who, in that wonderfully inclusive Greek way, let us join them for ouzo and octopus and conversation in good English (they had all been in the merchant navy and put in at the Clyde) and be late for lunch.

Such encounters became standard and perhaps the next day we met Desmond O'Grady, Irish poet, resident of Rome and summertime genius loci of Naoussa with the beautiful Florence, each day in a different long dress, their baby Leonardo and her sons Brian and

Mahlon. Since my father-in-law was the Scottish poet Hugh MacDiarmid there was that same felicitous connection that colours everything here. Just as in the second week Jack Grootendorst, calling in to pick up his newspaper from the Naoussa Hotel, discovered that the father of the Dutch family we were sitting with had been his fellow-student in Amsterdam. Jack and Maia and their daughters Sabina and Irena had just moved into the house they had built at Kolymbithres. He invited us all for dinner, picked us up in his speedboat and there we were, settled with holidays-for-life, histories and a first set of friends in the same accelerated, nailed-it-in-one, desperately uncool way that we had started out.

The Naoussa we found then was a fraction of the size it is now, dropping in a sharp triangle from the church on the hill, but as dazzling white as it is today. People painted the lines between the cobblestones and sang as they painted. The dustbin donkey in beaded headband and with green-painted oil cans slung either side was led through the harbour to round up the few blown away cigarette packets not immediately retrieved. When the donkey dropped its own trash that got swept up too. There were produce donkeys waiting below the steep outside staircases while housewives fetched change from the upper-storey houses which then made up the entire almost retail-free village. There was one clothes shop that sold corsets and bales of that sprigged black cotton that older women's dresses were made of. To buy newspapers, postcards, sun-screen, almost anything but food you went to Paroikia, which, when we visited, had just a handful of backpackers sitting at the ever-open seafront taverna, few of whom ever made their way to Naoussa.

Houses facing the square in Naoussa had back gardens stretching to the river, not yet encased in concrete. Inland from the bridge hens scratched and women washed clothes in the stream. The cafes in the square had an almost tangible men-only aura. Often, disconcertingly, glimpses of older worlds would break through the orthodoxies of this: a woman in a doorway spinning yarn with a distaff and spindle; a circus strong man in a leopard skin pulling a car through the square with a rope in his teeth; a Christ-like man, barefoot and in robes, passing through side-saddle on a donkey. We met students from Athens visiting their grandparents who told us that as children they had made the pre-tarmac journey from the port in donkey panniers. And in the evenings we met the few other foreigners at the café of Giorgos and Margarita on the harbour where our sons learned tavli.

We visited Lefkes where foreigners were rare enough for people to stop us and ask where we came from. We travelled on mules to the Valley of The Butterflies and the Convent of Christou tou Dassous where the nuns, skirts hitched up and perched on ladders to clean their chandeliers, chased us, or rather the mule driver who had brought us, off the premises with their feather dusters. We visited Naxos squatting in the bottom of a small boat around an immense custom-made white marble washbasin it was delivering. And when Yannis Papadakis extended his range we went in his boat to Delos where armed soldiers stepped forward to prevent us from disembarking. The Junta was still in power - some islands had the date of the coup, 21st April, etched out in giant letters on their marble mountainsides in the style of the white horses of the English chalk downs - and on the day we turned up Deputy Prime Minister Stylianos Pattakos was visiting the island with friends. We slunk off to Mykonos and came back later.

The following year Yannis was persuaded to take a small group to Santorini – an Italian geologist and his family, an American opera singer and hers, Desmond O'Grady and ourselves.
We arrived at the foot of the cliff staircase on a scorching hot day to find no mules waiting until someone spotted us from above and brought down three or four of those

unfortunate animals who carried us, two or three to a mule, to the top. We stayed overnight and had the square to ourselves at sundown as the other visitors returned to their cruise ships.

On a July morning in 1974 there were still only three or four families on Kolymbithres beach when we (family now complete with third-born) looked up to see the caique, not expected till one o'clock, pull in at the jetty. The captain waved and shouted something we couldn't make out but which made the others, all Greek, scramble to their feet and run to the boat. We scoured the heavens for thunder storms, mushroom clouds, angelic manifestations, then, still at a loss, scooped up the kids and ran after them On the boat a radio was playing martial music. We were adrift in a Graham Greene novel with no inkling of the plot.

Drawn up in the harbour area was a truck. In the back of it stood the young men of the village, some of them holding rifles. As it drew away their mothers lined the route and began to wail, some beating their breasts and tearing their hair. We were now in a Greek tragedy, hideously aware of our ignorance, anxious not to bother people so obviously in the grip of a life-altering crisis.

When we went to sit at a harbour ouzeria we were joined by other foreigners, all of us, in a news vacuum that is now hard to imagine, equally ignorant. Then Richard Winch arrived from the last boat out of Piraeus. Richard, an English television playwright, had in time past done his national service in army intelligence in Cyprus and had just flown in from London. His briefing was authoritative and alarming. The right-wing nationalist group EOKA B whose aim was to bring Cyprus under Greek rule had just staged a coup in Nikosia. Archbishop Makarios, President of Cyprus, had fled to London, Turkey had invaded Cyprus and Greece and Turkey were now on a war footing. As we digested that, questioned him and began to consider what the outcome might be we called for another carafe of ouzo. Then water. Sorry, they said. No water. The water plant guys had been called up.

At this point it seemed sensible to check out what practical expertise our small random group had to offer. We had none. Insubstantial parasitic stuff - journalism, real writing, film, illustration - was paying for our holidays. But on the matter of information we were thrice blest. There were on holiday in Naoussa at that time not one, not two, but three foreign correspondents all of whom were already trying to get off the island and go to Cyprus. The ferry operators, now on emergency orders to pick up islanders of call-up age, followed by, on subsequent runs, holidaying mainland Greek men, then their families, were unmoved by their sense of urgency. They had talked themselves into the main global hotspots but got nowhere with the Paroikia port police. So that evening we gathered around a short wave radio and a storm lantern on the terrace of the Naoussa Hotel (the island had gone for a total blackout) with Boris Kidell of the Observer, who had a house at Santa Maria, Andy Elten, Middle East Correspondent of Stern, and Olivier Todd of Nouvel Observateur.

Next day as they queued to wire disbelieving foreign editors behind local people sending birthday greetings we spent the morning at Piperi Beach (no more caiques) and in the afternoon, as I pushed my third-born in his buggy around the back of the village, I heard martial music still coming from the houses where people waited by their radios for news. As we passed one house a lady came out, handed my son a sprig of basil, and hugged us both in a we're-all-in-this-together sort of way.

In the evening, walking together through an altered and denuded village we saw a door in a high wall open and a lady we recognised as helping out at the Naoussa Hotel beckoned us in. There in the middle of the old village behind a wall and under a vine was a small farm - goats, hens, dogs, everything. Her husband and her grandson were there and brought out chairs for us and a carafe of their own ouzo, handing a glass to our 13-year-old, now ceremoniously up-graded to adulthood. We sat there, toasting each other, deploying our minimal Greek, powerfully moved not just by their kindness but by the instinctive nobility of the gesture, one we were often to find in similar circumstances, suggesting that the entire population of Paros could, if it arose, act out spontaneously and with gravitas anything by Aeschylus or Euiripedes. And this was all the more remarkable in that, from the Greek point of view, the Brits were questionable players in the affairs of Cyprus.

The foreign news contingent left, the crisis passed, the conscripts returned, and a week later the way was clear for ferries to take tourists to Piraeus. Jordanis got us a cabin on the Miaoulis and as we waited in the heat at Paroikia fishermen playing tavli on the deck of their boat beckoned to our by now accomplished older sons to join them.

So it was that the Junta fell and around the island smaller changes were taking place. Beach tavernas opened. Siesta hour softened. A retired Greek air force colonel taught our sons beach tennis. Local boys kicked footballs to them and shouted 'Glasgow Celtic'. They kicked them back and shouted 'Panathenaikos. A new kind of coffee appeared: Café Nes was offered here and there; and the choice of wines - Retsina, Pavros Mavro, Demestika – that so upset French visitors was replaced by increasingly new and interesting local labels as well as the 'open wines' of the tavernas.

Television arrived. My husband Mike and Richard Winch spent a whole day helping Jordanis to fix a roof aerial to the hotel so that they could watch the Olympic Games, their reward being endless unedited coverage of Bulgarian women shot-putters.

(Richard's wife Phoebe, marooned with their children on the day of the coup in a hotel at Piraeus that turned out to be a brothel, arrived later and had become a close friend.) Legeris and Zabbeta Vionis who had run the most popular restaurant in the village opened the Minoa Hotel in what was then the edge of the countryside and we started staying there.

Backpackers came increasingly to Naoussa, tried sleeping on the beach, and were discouraged. Not so easily discouraged was the practice of toplessness. When that extended to Kolymbithres, a family beach, notices appeared in the village – I have one still – depicting a nude man with horns and cloven hooves leading his helpless unclothed family to damnation on a public beach. Tourist police were, briefly, despatched to Kolymbithres to ask people to cover up - this, perhaps, not a thought-through solution since toplessness is an exclusively female crime and the tourist police were male. A French girl sunbathing next to us was asked by a policeman to put her bikini top back on. Impossible, she said. She hadn't brought it. Well then, he said, you must put on your dress. Impossible. She hadn't come on holiday to sit on the beach in a dress. OK, he said, show me your passport. Passport? Impossible. Passport, he insisted. Where, she said, raising her arms and inviting him to check out her purse, sandals and tiny folded dress, might she be hiding a passport?

The Satanic sunbather . . . I took down the notice from the lamppost and kept it because it spoke of things unarticulated and deeply foreign to a Protestant non-believer from the north-west fringe of Europe . . . of entities who watch, Dionysian as well as Satanic, Olympian along with celestial, and those in between like the Muses waiting in the hills above Paroikia for the young cow-herd Archilochus to exchange his beast for a lyre. There are other dimensions here, other ways of thinking and being. Open yourself to them and Paros throbs with possibilities.

That so much of the past remains to be discovered is one of the thrills of being here. When Othon Kaparis, Naoussa doctor and amateur archaeologist, told us he had found pottery shards in the hills above Kolymbithres . . when Dimitris Schiliardi excavated the site of the Mycenean acropolis there and we climbed up to watch the excavations . . . when I see on a still day the grooves cut into the rocks in the shallows of Naoussa bay or the shoreline of Santa Maria, or pick up a pottery shard in my garden. . . then the open, inclusive and incomplete history of Paros is at its most bewitching.

Much of our outsider experience of Paros is comparative, but surely the greater part of it is constant. The older redoubtable travellers we met in our first years who had found the island the hard way were themselves only the latest in the long line of people, stretching back to antiquity, who had stepped ashore and liked what they saw. The pageant continues. The island has changed, but then it always did. You are always a newcomer however long you have been coming, but equally – and I think this is a special quality of Paros – you feel an immediate sense of recognition. Your welcome is unconditional and intense as if you were always destined to come here and swell the cast of the island, for this episode and perhaps the next.

Deirdre Grieve
Glasgow, Scotland
January, 2012

Desmond O'Grady's poem "The Olive at Ambilas".
Courtesy of Annelize Goedbloed

SABINE'S STORY · 1969
By Sabine Grootendorst

Sabine and Dimitris in 1974

A little story of love for Paros and a little love story.

A couple of nights ago I dreamt of Florence Tamburro – don't remember the theme but I had a good feeling about it - who is a friend of mine and of my late parents. For me Florence is an essential part of Paros, whether we talk about forty-five years ago or about today. The dream reminded me of the fact that I had promised to contribute to the Parian stories and I realized that I still had done absolutely nothing about it. Not even given it a thought. The email-request was just lying there on my desk somewhere hidden in the endless pile of "must do"- things. Well, that dream made me finally sit down and think how to write some kind of story that will be a coherent personal account of my early days on Paros and will be readable. The coherent part is trouble, since there are just too many crossroads of memories. I will give it a try though! My sister, Irene, will be writing her own story too so there might be some similarities, but that should be all right.

I first stepped on the island in 1969, was ten years old and came with my parents. They, Jack and Maja, had come for the first time in 1965 or 1966 and stayed at the only hotel in Naoussa available (with running water AND electricity!) named an original 'Hotel Naoussa' and which was managed by the Maroulidi family. They spoke English and Jordanis (the father) helped my parents out with the communication.

My parents fell in love with the island, the bay of Naoussa, the sun, the village of Naoussa and the walk around the bay towards Kolybithres and Ag. Ioannis. The climate, the Aegean light, warm sea and the music were additional reasons for their love. I guess the food was too, since Maja made it an issue to cook something Greek once a week ever since their first visit! During one of their daily walks around the bay from Naoussa to Kolybithres they found a little spot with a hidden beach that stole their hearts. They both had the wish to buy some land there and build a house. They did! This beach would be called Jack's beach later, then it turned into Sabina's and Dimitris' beach, Irene and Peter's beach and hopefully this beach will eventually be called Irini's, (our daughter) Zoe's and Elina's beach (Irene and Peter's daughters).

The building of the house started in 1967 but was stopped because my parents were not very happy with the new military regime that had installed itself (was installed? but no politics in this story!) in Greece and they both were doubtful whether or not to continue their project. In the meantime, everybody up North in Germany was thinking Maja and Jack had totally lost it by building a summerhouse not only so far away in Greece, but even on an isolated island!! Thank god, however, they proceeded with materializing their dream and the house was finished by the summer of 1968. That same year our family moved from Germany to Holland so my sister and I were sent to our Dutch grandparents to learn Dutch instead of having a first summer in Paros! But the next year I finally could come and see for myself what my parents had been so delirious about for the past four years. I only had seen some 8mm films made by Jack, to give the kids some impressions, but that was all. I do, however, remember definitely looking forward to a see a sea that was actually blue and not the black/gray colors of the seas in Northern Europe.

So, summer 1969 was my first time on Paros. After a pretty tiring but adventurous trip on the "Elly" ferry boat of seven hours from Piraeus, we finally arrived at this beautiful spot in the middle of the Aegean. I was impressed by the beauty, and maybe already then, at ten years of age, I realized that Paros actually was the center of the Earth ... (I am certainly convinced of it now at fifty-three!). My sister and I arrived with Jack, my grandmother and Jack's sister. Maja was not with us due to university obligations. So there we were, trying to get from Paroikia to Kolybithres -five persons - which was quite an enterprise in those days since there were about three taxis on the whole island. Eventually, we came to the house after a couple of hours with a swearing and sweating taxi driver who feared his car was ruined because of the terrible dirt road (naming it a dirt road is an over-statement as the road was just a wide donkey path!)

Taking into consideration that we were up on that day of arrival at around 4.30 a.m. to catch the boat at 7 to Paros, (no, I am not kidding, Jack was quite neurotic about being on time and would turn into a total tyrant if the kids were too slow, which we were, of course, at 4.30 a.m.). So being quite tired, my first impressions were these: very lousy and moody taxi drivers (things haven't changed much for that matter), very hot, very far away and "what do you mean Dad? No electricity? No telephone? No mail for my weekly comic book? And no hot water???????" Coming from a nice area in Holland and being a spoiled brat, these were things I had a bit of a hard time to deal with in the beginning, but slowly all these "disasters" turned into wonderful adventures. I must give my parents credit for that. All the things that were not available were turned into challenges in Kolybithres. No problems, just challenges! Reading with oil lamps and playing family games around the table in candlelight was quite something else. No water? No problem ... go to the beach, fetch water and flush the toilet!

Being spoiled really meant the fact that I actually was given the chance in life to go every summer and spend six weeks in paradise! But this awareness came somewhat later in life!

Back to the first summer and back to complaining: we also did not have a car, which was a bummer since we lived on the opposite side of the bay of Naoussa and did shopping with a dingy (by the time we reached the harbor of Naoussa we would be soaked!

Another disaster…) or on Jack's little ancient motor bike that was called Rolls Royce, which it was of course, considering there was no other way to get around the bay, except on foot. No boats transporting tourists across the bay yet. Another little disaster, in my opinion, was having to do the dishes (an everyday argument with my sister about whose turn it was!) but the real horror was the "cooking" of our dirty underwear in this big pot on the stove! This was total hardship! Especially washing the soap out of that laundry in the river together with other villagers, a total embarrassment. I am sooooo happy with electricity and a washing machine nowadays.

I have been gibbering about what I did **not have** the first couple of weeks because it was bit of a culture shock to me (but hey, I was ten. Is that an excuse?) However, slowly all these things "missing" were forgotten somehow and replaced by the enormous amount of things which I **did** have: like the sun forever shining, swimming to the little island in the bay, snorkeling, a wonderful beach and sea just in front of my bedroom, playing with the boat, walking and exploring the amazingly beautiful beaches, finding shells and stones I had never ever seen before (or an occasional skeleton of a goat!) listening to island or classical music on our terrace on a sun lounger with a blanket around me in the evening looking at an incredible clear amount of stars, so close that you thought of walking up the mountain and touching them!. A moon so clear and big, that it almost became daylight, a cold daylight but turning warmer when the moon would "lose" parts of the cheek again. All these were new and a great experiences that obviously never let me go. Even cooking dirty underwear was part of a routine I eventually got used to.

Back to the first summer. The only other house on our side of the bay was the farm up hill (Pantelia and Manolis Katakouzinos were the farm-family my parents bought the land from) another farm towards Ag. Ioannis near bamboo-beach and the Monastery of Ag. Ioannis that was inhabited by a Dutch painter, Gisele, for six months of the year. She actually turns one hundred this year, God willing.

The farmhouse up the hill was big fun! Lots of animals to chase and we played with the youngest children of the farmers or their grandchildren. We would go up every day and get fresh milk that had to be boiled.! Another new experience. In Holland milk was not boiled anymore since ages since all milk was coming out of ready-to-drink bottles there. Thank God, Mom had a different pot for that!). So milk- boiling became another obligation Irene and I had arguments about whose turn it was. But it soon all became part of the daily routine (including the arguments of course!)

Some of the farm daughters (they had five daughters, which would have meant their bankruptcy, were it not for my parents who bought some land so they could pay for the dowries). I remember that Maja would bring a full suitcase year after year with clothing, shoes and a case of cutlery for yet another wedding of another daughter. Seeing children in the village wearing my old clothes and shoes, did plunge me into realization that not everybody in this world had the same privileges as I had. And I am glad that I realized this, because some people never get to that point, unfortunately.

The sea, the beaches and the farm were our playgrounds for the first years. The farm was always full of people and animals, the chickens would walk around the two roomed farmhouse and so did the donkeys. Speaking of which, one beautiful morning that first summer I helped the son of the farmer, Kostas, out on the threshing floor hitting the behinds of the donkeys with a bamboo stick trying to make them move forwards in circles to thresh the hay. This hay was "aired" with a big hay fork that ended up – during a very unfortunate movement of the fork held by Kostas and me not watching - into my leg. Screams, hysteria all over, the whole family around me, screaming in Greek and me not able to walk or talk anymore. Big drama! Big and loud screams! Pantelia, the grand farm lady, almost killed her son who had worked with the hayfork for not watching out. I will spare you the details of how I got down to my house, - Jack not being there (gone shopping with Rolls Royce) - my grandmother (a former nurse) trying to calm the whole Katakouzinos family down in Dutch and they just kept calling for the Holy Virgin in Greek. A perfect Greek hysterical drama scene the moment my father entered the house wondering what the f.--k was going on! This was one of the rare moments in my life that I saw my father very upset and not knowing what to do. Doctor or no doctor? If yes, how to get there with me not able to walk etc. etc. Eventually he took Rolls Royce again, picked up a taxi in Naoussa and had him drive back to Kolybithres. Finally, in the late afternoon we got to Paroikia and found the one and only doctor on the island Dr. Kebabbis. He, of course, asked whether or not I had had a Tetanus shot before coming to Paros. Jack naturally did not know this and of course there was no way of finding out since there was no phone available at the time that would automatically dial our home in Holland, and ask Maja if I had had this vaccination. So I had this Tetanus shot anyway, a stitch in my leg and the next thing you know while driving back home, I am throwing up all over the taxi car with fever and trying to hold up a very nasty diarrhea attack. I spared the taxi that. Result: I had Tetanus, (diagnosed by my grandmother) since Maja was thoughtful enough to give us Tetanus vaccinations before going to a faraway spot like Greece, a country full of hay forks! It is not a good thing to get two Tetanus shots within one month. So we learned. I could not swim for three weeks and I was not happy.

But then the next summers many things were getting better and better: I was twelve going on eighteen and looked it! I met all the kids of the friends my parents had made during the previous summers. Mahlon and Brian, sons of Florence, Mark and Henry

Emanuel, Joshua de Carlo and Aaron Zajac. On all these lovely boys I had a crush at one point or another.

Ambelas taverna and Damianos were discovered and we kids were allowed to come along (and sleep in Jack's jeep, if tired). Of course we never slept in the jeep, tired or not. Our parents had lost the plot of bed-time tyranny all together, so we would just stay on the beach in Ambelas and do our own thing. We had changed playground .... Like, bringing bottles and bottles and bottles of ice cold (and therefore drinkable) Retsina from Damianos' fridge, going to the beach and getting wasted. Smoking and getting drunk for the first time, getting stoned for the first time, swimming naked for the first time and so on. When I come to think of it, most of the un-puritan things in life I did for the first time on Paros). Our parents never knew a thing (or so we thought) in those days; they were too busy with their own fun and flirtations so we had ours. I had a ball and this continued for the summers to come.

The year of 1974 was a major change for Paros and me. Greece regained her democracy and I lost my virginity. In 1973 already, my eye had fallen on a Greek guy whom I heard playing guitar and singing the stars out of the sky (this is actually a Dutch expression, but you will get the grip!) and in 1974 we were together with the "parea" of Aliki Maroulidi. (Aliki was my chaperone together with my sister that summer). At one point I finally got my parents to allow me to go to Naoussa <u>alone</u> – without my sister - and pretend to go out with Aliki. I had secretly arranged with Dimitri, with whom I officially was going out by now, that I could sleep at his house that night. I was very exited about it but unfortunately it was the very same day that the military regime decided to invade Cyprus and everybody was mobilized and going crazy. Dimitris, in those days politically very active, was all over the place and was not particularly interested in my plans for that day/night at the time. That same morning I was in the village buying bread for Maja, who had arranged lunch for many friends. All of a sudden, there was this panic everywhere! I could not possibly get a boat back home across the bay and was very worried about the hurricane (called Maja) that would await me for not being on time with the bread for lunch. But what could I do? I was looking for Dimitris (I mean, we had a date tonight and who cares about invasions of Cyprus and mobilizations in the end!) I could not find him. Thought he had been mobilized as well, together with Stavros and Panajiotis, his buddies from old times, who were actually in the army in those days. The whole village was in a total panic and I was too, but obviously for very different reasons! Eventually. I found my father who was in charge of getting people to the ferry boats in order to leave. Jack still was one of the few that actually had a car back then. He brought me home with the bread on time!!! I do not remember what became of the lunch, however, I do remember walking back to Naoussa around the bay after lunch in order to find Dimitris, which I eventually did.

Well that night was special ... for Greece and for me!

I was totally in love with Dimitris, the guitar player (and I was not the only one, he obviously was very popular!). We had endless discussions and talks, also on politics, but that was still a subject I was not really able to grasp and discuss at the age of fifteen. But I just loved it and I sucked up every new theory I heard. Eventually, at the end of the day, however, I still was a very young, high-school girl living in Holland and Dimitris was a student in Greece three thousand miles away. These were not very good ingredients to keep a love story going. By the end of the year 1976, we ended this very beautiful but somehow complicated and impossible love affair.

Over the years he got married and divorced and so did I (with/from different persons!). After several detours and ten years later we hooked up together again and decide to give it a go in 1986. I moved to Greece in that year and I am happy to write that we are still together after so many years. We have a daughter, Irini, who loves Paros as much as we do. Our daughter is befriended with the children of Nikitas, Nikos, Aliki etc. etc. and hopefully their children will continue to be friends as well. I see my daughter having the same kind of fun we had, (dancing all through the night and seeing the sun go up over Naxos!). Us in Ambelas, Irini clubbing with much more choices for hang-outs nowadays. A lot has changed since the 70s but it is still the island of Paros with its special magnetic atmosphere that brings so many people back to it again and again.

If I had only one day left in my life and could make a wish, I would choose to sit all day on Jack's beach in front of the house, watching the sun set behind the hill giving the red light over Naoussa, being in peace. That's all I would ask for!

I want to end this little story of love for Paros and little love story by saying that first of all I think that I was lucky to actually marry the love of my life and who also is the man of my life. This just rarely happens to a woman. And second, a very fortunate fact is that Paros is still both his and my center of the world!

Sabine Grootendorst
Athens, Greece
March 201

Captain Leonardo.
Courtesy of Florence Tamburro

IRENE'S STORY · 1969
By Irene Grootendorst

Irene with her donkey

I don't think I have ever been as excited as on the day I first travelled to Greece. It was July 1969. For over a year I've been ticking off the days on a chart behind my bed, until finally the day had come: We were going to Greece as a family because the house on Paros was finished...at last.

My sister Sabine and I were boiling over with excitement. I didn't know where to look when we arrived in Athens, everything looked so spectacularly different. I loved the chaos, the loud people, the honking cars and the big buildings that were so crammed full of lamps they looked like giant Christmas trees. The traffic and the thousands of cars, motorbikes and green put-puts was something completely alien to me. A special treat were the yellow electric trolleys that got stuck on the road and sat there like fat insects while the crowd tried to attach their feelers back to the suspended electric wiring. I thought it was hilarious and I enjoyed watching the crowds go crazy. My father Jack, on the other hand, was swearing in the front seat of the taxi (patience was not one of his strong points).

We stayed overnight at the King Minos hotel on Omonia Square. I remember the friendly porter (he'd still be there many years later). He looked like the late King Hussein of Jordan and always had a smile on his face. I loved hanging over the balcony looking at all the hustle and bustle in Omonia Square. What an exciting city!! A whole different world had opened up to me, a stark contrast to the green leafy suburb we came from, not a sound to be heard there after 7pm.

I loved going for a walk around the centre of Athens. Jack was getting his shoes shined once a year. One day we went into a shop because Jack needed a hat. After paying for the hat Jack fumbled with it to remove a label that was irritating him. By the time we made it to the exit of the shop Jack had ripped the hat to pieces and threw it in the bin, much to the astonishment of the shopkeeper who stared at us with open mouth. I also loved the coins with the holes in them. You could buy 'tzikla' by the piece…it made the budget last much longer. And then there were the sesame bars with sticky honey. I loved the new world of candy.

Then the day came to go to Paros. That morning we took a taxi to Piraeus which was only half an hour drive. Jack, however, chased us all into a taxi one and a half hours before as he was the biggest travelling stress-head; and you never know we might get stuck behind one of those insects with loose feelers again and miss the ferry. A couple of years later I sat in the back of this same taxi- ride contemplating my funeral because I realised I left my braces in the napkin at the breakfast area of the hotel. One way or another, I had to tell Jack that we had to go back to find my braces. Sadly, there was only that nuclear option available to me. I survived. I think we went back but couldn't find my braces, still made the ferry of course because we had left way too early (sometimes being over-cautious has its merits and my sister has since taken over the let's-get-stressed-'cause-we're-travelling role).

I loved the ferry. Her name was Elli, and I could lean against the railing for hours, staring at the water feeling the sun beaming down on me (also in short supply in our leafy green suburb). It was always such an enjoyable part of the slow trip to Paros (until my mother Maja, Biz Buin 9 in hand, called me into the shade).

After we'd arrived in Paros and we were driving on the dirt road towards our house my mind was running through the films again which my parents had shown me of Greece. The images were full of green hills with lots of trees and caves to hide in. It would be the perfect place to play cowboys and robbers. We drove passed the farm behind our house and the farmer's whole family ran out to welcome us. It was my first of many encounters with the warmth and friendliness of the Greek people.

When we entered the house I didn't know what to think. It was a big white slab of marble with minimum furniture and not a cave or tree in sight. The lonely mulberry tree next to Marousso's farm on the way to Ag.Ioannis definitely wasn't going to cut it. When I asked where the hills, trees and caves were I was told I was probably referring to footage from Naxos. How were we supposed to play my favourite game in this barren environment? Except for three distant farms, there was nothing around us, certainly no greenery. Clearly, we were on the wrong island! As it turned out, the farm behind our house was the perfect place to play and although the farmer's granddaughter was a bit older than I she was happy to spend time with me. I still see the back of the farm, a symbol of my happy childhood, every day on a painting by Mike Brady that is hanging in our dining room.It didn't take long for me to fall in love with the house, the area, the island.

The first summer my grandmother and aunt (Jack's mother and sister) joined us. Maja came later as she still had to teach at university. I remember it wasn't always easy running the household the first years. Water had to be boiled and cooled before consumption, all washing had to be done by hand and there was no electricity. One summer the water shortage was so bad we had to carry the dishes to the beach and wash them in seawater. Our stove and fridge worked with gas bottles that had to be purchased in Naoussa. When Jack tried, in his best Greek, to explain he wanted a gas bottle, saying "butan" and waving his arms in a round motion, the local fishermen thought he wanted a 'putana' and suggested he try Piraeus. Jack's Greek never really took off and remained limited to "ego pame pipi" when he needed a toilet, "Kalo taxidi" when starting a meal and "Kali orexi" when saying goodbye. Maja did a much better job, she was very studious and practised her heavily accented Greek whenever possible. The irony of course was that Jack was the better communicator.

At my first birthday party in Paros I turned eight. It was one of the most exciting parties I can remember. My parents had stumbled upon a group of hippies from San Francisco that were camping in Kolymbithris amongst the rocks and had invited them over to the house to celebrate with us. One of the hippies had carved a little wooden statue for me, which showed an American Indian head on one side and on the other a mermaid. My own little netsuke! I still have it and I cherish it. Polly and Warwick where there and Warwick had painted toothpaste all over his chest, looking very exotic, and played the bagpipes and we all danced around him on the terrace, with our oil lamps flickering in the dark here and there. There were lots of other people whom I can't remember but it was the party of my life. All the parties were fun though, especially my birthday parties. For my ninth birthday Desmond wrote me a beautiful poem for which I had no appreciation at the time but it's also on our wall now and I always get emotional when I read it.

We all enjoyed the challenges and adventures. At least I think we all did. I'm not sure about my grandmother who was yelled at by Jack for leaving the flimsy skin on the milk after boiling it. Yes, it was the end of the world according to Jack. I also remember my aunt doing a tribal dance on the dinner table because there was a mouse in the house (again my sister has since taken up this role). The incident of Sabine getting a hay fork in her thigh while helping on the farm took years off my grandmother's life. I still see her screaming, with shampoo in her hair, giving orders on how best to transport my sister back to the house and to the doctor. Grandma was good at giving orders; she was a nurse after all.

I just loved everything about the house, the country, the farm and its animals and especially the warmth and generosity of the people. I loved the food too; everything was fresh, and tasted so beautifully. Some products took a bit of getting used to and some choices were limited. Soft drinks were either portokalada or limonada with its only distinguishing feature being the colour because it was just sugar water that made the enamel crack off your teeth. Eggs, cheese, milk and butter (a lump of rancid glue) we bought from the farm as well as tomatoes and other vegetables. If anyone in Paros still has the original tomatoes and seeds that existed in the 60s, please tell me.

We also all soon developed an ear for Greek music. In no time I knew all the island songs - ballos, sirtaki and tsifteteli - off by heart, without having the slightest idea what I was singing. 'Maria me ta kitrina' was my favourite, which I sang together with Maja and Sabine. Jack stuck to blasting 'Delilah' alongside Tom Jones while scrubbing the terrace.

Another party at the house ended with Jack generously giving everybody a ride back to Naoussa in his red speedboat. He must have gone back and forth a lot of times and every time after the party-goers stumbled out of the boat in Naoussa harbour, he went full throttle back to Kolymbithris to get the next lot. Shortly after, Jack was summoned to the harbour master to explain what he was thinking when waking up half the village at 5am.

We saw a lot of the Irish crowd too (my Irish song repertoire expanded as well) especially Desmond, Florence and little Leonardo. Sabine hung out more with Brian and Mahlon but I enjoyed spending time teaching Leonardo to jump off the rocks in front of our house and pull urchin pins out of his foot when he had jumped the wrong way. I remember Florence as this smiling, dancing, amazing looking woman (she always wore such beautiful dresses – her wavy blue one was my favourite). As a matter of fact, she is my idol. She is in her 80s, travels the world, has a great relationship with her children, wonderful friends, and is still this smiling, dancing, amazing looking woman with always an interesting story to tell. I'll sign up for that.

I only have to walk through my house and look at items that bring back memories. A painting by Dieter Kopp that he gave me for my birthday. He was a German artist who lived with his daughter Laura in Rome and when he came to Paros they first lived in a cave outside Naoussa on the way to Langeri. I thought it was just the coolest thing to live with your dad in a cave. Dieter had a girlfriend from Montevideo and we became friends and pen-pals for many years to come.

One night Maja and Jack went to Ta Fikia, a tavern at the turnoff to Kolymbithris. It was run by Jordanis and Maria, who became family friends. On a windless night you could hear the music as if it was next door. It was here that the whole family learnt to dance balos and sirtaki. They had a jukebox and you could eat and dance all night. That one night Sabine and I decided to have our own party at home and danced on the terrace, loudly blowing whistles. We forgot that the whistle was a distress sign and the farmer and his wife were asked to come to the house if they ever heard the whistle. After fifteen minutes of partying, all of a sudden Manoli and his wife Pandelia stood on our terrace in their pyjamas and sleeping hats (I thought these things only existed in fairy tales). Our parents brought us to the farm the next day and we had to mumble an apology with hanging heads.

The other exciting place to party was Ambelas. It had only one tavern and it belonged to Damianos, the best solo dancer on the island and one of Jack's best friends. He had a jukebox, a few tables and a dance floor. Mostly he had Greek 78" records but some of them were 'modern songs'. Sabina's and my favourite song was in slot G4, which was

"Venus" by Shocking Blue. As soon as the music stopped, we raced to the jukebox to press G4, and the other number for "Yellow River". How many nights we spent partying there! It still is one of my favourite spots, even if it has gone chic and no crazy things happen there anymore and not near enough dancing!

In the early days sometimes I got tired while we all partied in Ambelas. When I did, I slept in the back of our jeep. When it was time to drive home I climbed on Jack's lap in the driver's seat. I claimed he was far too drunk to drive home. Maja couldn't drive a manual so I felt very mature driving the family home safely on Jack's lap. The team effort worked like this: Jack thought he had control over the accelerator and clutch, I firmly had control over the gear stick and the steering wheel, and this is how, from the age of twelve, I drove home on numerous nights when dawn was just around the corner. I knew every hump, bump, rock and bend between Ambelas and our house. Sometimes we made stops to dispose of hitchhikers in various states of disrepair. As irresponsible as this may now sound (even though ours was the only car on the road), it was great and I loved it.

Pandelia, the farmer's wife, opened a tavern in Kolymbithris right on the water's edge. It was the most magical spot and sadly it has been completely derelict for many years now. The daughters cooked and the food was always delicious and fresh. We spend so many afternoons eating, drinking and playing music there. I think it was at Pandelia's tavern that I saw Dimitri, Sabine's husband, for the first time playing his guitar and singing to the crowd's delight. Pandelia ran a tight ship with the tavern. Huge iceblocks were delivered by the fisherman to keep the fridge cold. Octopi were hanging out to dry on the washing line between the kitchen and the toilet. On windless days you could hear her scream across the bay to her daughter Flora to bring some more 'psomiiiiiiiiiiiiii'. I don't know how she managed to yell across the bay but that woman managed a number of incredible things. She only died a couple of years ago....we thought she would bury us all.

I loved going to the village across the bay. Naoussa still has a beautiful platia and the harbour is heritage protected. The little church opposite the Venetian ruins was our changing room when our dingy was our mode of transport because we all inevitable arrived soaking wet. The only tables I remember in the harbour were those of Stratis' ouzeri and the kafenion of Margarita and George. The crowds were nothing like they are now but it is still beautiful. When I was little, the shops were basic and tiny. I watched the village women wash their clothes in the creek that still runs behind the plateia. The post office consisted of Dimestoklis sitting in a minute shop on the Plateia with a shoebox full of letters on his lap. It took forever for him to meticulously go through the shoebox, looking through his inch-thick glasses to see whether any mail had arrived for us. Often the first journey of the letter was to get into Dimestoklis' shoebox, the second was doing the rounds through Naoussa because someone was going to give the mail to someone who was going to meet someone later who would give us our mail. This process easily took the same amount of time as the trip from Holland to Greece. Another shop was that of Constantza on the harbour. She knitted beautiful, but very scratchy, jumpers. She was the mother of Jack's goddaughter who since has opened a restaurant there.

One of my fondest memories is when we fell asleep to the sound of Vivaldi's Four Seasons while lying on the terrace with the whole family and watching the stars, counting the falling stars until I fell into a slumber and Jack had to carry me to bed. It's no longer possible to watch the stars, there is too much light pollution. Years later Sabine and I sometimes joined Stavros and Nikitas on their fishing trips and we lay on the nets watching the stars and singing songs. I loved being on a boat – any boat – and I could ride up and down with Pippis and Michaelis from Naoussa to Kolymbithris and back all day, together with Leonardo who had also developed a taste for this!

On my tenth birthday I finally was given the birthday present I had pestered my parents about for years: A donkey. It belonged to Manoli the farmer and they had agreed that my parents could buy the donkey and its saddle and that I would use the donkey in summer and then it would go back to the farm. Before I was allowed to come out of my room, I remember Sabine saying to me, with the biggest grin, that I was going to be sooooooo happy with my birthday present. When I saw the donkey on the terrace it took my brain a while to kick into gear and realise that my dream had come true. I was so happy I thought my heart would burst out of my chest. From then on I rode Marika up and down Mount Vigla behind our house; I rode to Naoussa and did the shopping not only for my family but also for Gisele who lived in the Monastery at Ag.Ioannis. I loved going through the small streets of Naoussa and getting the melons and tomatoes from Pippis, one of the few shops still remaining in its original spot. When I was finished, I treated myself to a risogalo at Georgios and Christos' kafenion on the harbour while Marika my donkey was tied up at the door. Margarita, Georgios's wife, made the second best risogalos (the best ones were Koula's, Dimitris' mother).

We developed wonderful friendships in our early years in Paros that would last a lifetime. Of the friends so dear to me are Alexandra and Heiner. I remember Alexandra and I followed a little fishing boat that was catching octopus on a windless night outside our house. We just kept following it in the direction of Ag.Ioannis until we realised we had walked a long way from home, it was pitch black and although finding our way home was only a matter of following the coast line back, it was still rather scary but very adventurous. I can't remember how impressed our parents were about our disappearing for so long (if they even noticed...) but it's a very fond memory.

One afternoon when it was time to leave Paros again for the year (which inevitably involved tears) we set out to board a derelict ferry called the Kyklades. It didn't start well because Jack and the jeep were refused boarding because of bad weather so it was just Maja, Sabine and I. The trip was horrendous. It must have been 8 or 9 Beaufort and it took nine hours instead of six. I remember Maja spent the entire time on a stool with her head in a bucket. I tried to sleep and ignore the putrid smell and I don't remember what Sabine was doing but I remember her telling Maja that she just got her periods for the first time. The expression on Maja's face was priceless.

We rarely ventured into Paroikia, the main town on the island. Maybe it's the wrong impression but I always had the idea that the Paroikia crowd was more foreign artists who stuck together and the Naoussa crowd was mixing more with the locals.
The general consensus was that Paroikia was overrun with tourists and far too noisy. Desmond aptly named the main tourist track through Paroikia 'Fifth Avenue'. There was this rivalry between Naoussa and Paroikia that exists between New York and LA, Sydney and Melbourne, Amsterdam and Rotterdam. To this day I still meet people from 'the other side' who have been on Paros since the 60s and 70s. How is that possible?

In the summer of 1974 the Cyprus crisis hit and I remember lots of people screaming and crying and everyone in Paros with a car was summoned to drive young men suitable to join the army to Paroikia, to catch the boat to wherever they needed to be to save Greece from a terrible disaster. I was too young to understand any of it but the sudden change in energy and vibe and the fear on people's faces will always stay with me
 I also remember Sabine being very upset because the love of her life was also being whisked away (there was always the suspicion of course that Jack had a hand in the crisis to avert the crisis of his daughter going out with the guy with the big moustache and the

guitar....joke!). She only just started going out with Dimitri that summer and was madly in love.

As I got older and wanted to venture out on my own my donkey came in handy again. It was the summer I would turn fifteen and my best friend Claudia and I had nine weeks in Paros. We were allowed to go out a few nights a week. When we weren't allowed out we often saddled up my donkey and left her behind our house. We kissed our parents good night in our pyjamas, only to jump back into our clothes, hop out the window, onto my donkey and ride into the exciting nightlife of Naoussa. By that time a few more places had opened up, like Klimataria on the Plateia and Windmills behind the big church. We tied the poor donkey to the door of the 'disco' and when we had finished dancing our hearts out we fell asleep against each other in the saddle and woke up when Marika came to a sudden halt because we were in front of our house. The poor animal, I'm sure I've taken years of her life. It didn't take long for her to work out what the nightly trips were all about and the ride into Naoussa always took considerably longer than the ride home.

When Marika wasn't our mode of transport we often crashed in the laundry of Hotel Naoussa, courtesy of Aliki, who on many occasions sneaked us in when we were too tired to walk home. So often we'd spend hours contemplating how to get home. Could we ask one of the fishermen to ferry us across the bay? Shall we ask Aliki? Who has a car? (Nobody did, except the ones who thought we were asleep in our beds). If we had spent the same time moving our legs, we would have been home three times by then. How envious I was of our friends who had the good fortune of having sensible parents that had thought of staying in a house in the middle of Naoussa, a stone's throw from the clubs, instead of staying in godforsaken Kolimbithris. I feel ashamed to admit that Claudia and I once 'borrowed' a bike to get home in the early hours. We brought it back the next morning but unfortunately it belonged to a friend of a good family friend and it didn't take this family friend long to figure out who had 'borrowed' the bike. Of course I denied any knowledge. To this day, every time I see him I think of the bike incident and that I should 'fess up.....he probably has forgotten all about it. A year later my school friend Pita joined me in Paros and we had so much fun. Every summer is different and has its special memories. We spent a week in Naxos and we both ventured out tasting what the beginnings of love life was all about.

I nagged Maja and Jack into going to Paros in the winter of '77-78 because I wanted to catch up with my friends and boyfriend. We had glorious weather and it was only my second time in Paros in winter and I loved it. The light was so different and the atmosphere and the mood of the locals differed to that in summer. The day we were about to leave the weather turned sour and we were stuck in Paros, staying on the Elli for a whole week (it was more comfortable than our house). My parents were getting frustrated with the delay, especially Jack who was supposed to be sworn in as a Member of Parliament. I loved the adventure of being trapped on the island and missing a week of school. We went from house to house, keeping warm and joining the locals making the best of it.

Especially during the 70s Paros created the perfect counter-balance to our structured life in the Netherlands. In the Netherlands Jack was the businessman, Mum the university lecturer and Sabine and I were growing up in a posh suburban villa, attending our decent school.
It was beautiful, safe and quiet and I have very happy memories of it and I made my best friends for life during that period. But then....Paros was free, crazy, unstructured, loud, impulsive, it was filled with music and dance and we were surrounded by different friends from all walks of life. It made life definitely more colourful and so much more

interesting and I'll be forever grateful to Maja and Jack for taking the plunge and buying land from Manolis the farmer who needed cash for the dowry of his daughter, and to build the house in Kolymbithris.

The island really started changing in the 80s. Many more tourists came, money started to pour in from the European Union and slowly Greece as a whole started to change. Things disappeared, like the red corals I saw snorkelling in front of our house and the personal friendships that grew between visitors and the locals. Hotels mushroomed out of the ground, but thankfully high-rise buildings have never been allowed. I probably also noticed the changes more as I was a young adult by that time. An airport was built, which made travelling to the island quicker and did away with the need of an overnight stay in Athens.

As Desmond predicted in his poem for my ninth birthday:

> *When your next decade comes around*
>
> *Much will be changed here, forgotten, drowned*
>
> *In the sea by the god of money*
>
> *That will surely come like the last meltemi.*

As young adults we still would spend pretty much every summer in Paros, joining Maja and Jack with friends and boyfriends. Sabine and Dimitri had split up years earlier and I was devastated at the time, convinced that these two people belonged together. I was too young to realise that they both needed a detour to make it work in the end.

Losing Jack in 1986 was a big blow. Luckily, we had had a couple of great summers when we had sailed with him through the Kyklades on his dream sailing boat the Meltemi. One summer Jack and I ventured out together on the boat and we got into trouble. We got stuck in a combination of engine failure, not a breath of wind, a huge swell and only sand beneath us so the anchor would not catch: every sailor's nightmare. I wasn't scared until I saw the fear on Jack's face. He ended up sending a may-day call and help came not long before the yacht would have smashed against the rocks near Sifnos. It was a small Greek navy ship that towed us to . Syros.

After Jack died, the three girls just pulled together and we took care of the house as best as we could. Sabine had in the meantime moved to Athens because she'd married Dimitri (told you!), I had moved to Australia and joined up with Peter whom I met in Athens in 1984 when I was studying at the Athens Centre, and Maja remained in the Canal house in Amsterdam. Although we were far away from each other, the house has always kept the family together. I'm sure I have had more quality time with Maja and Sabine because I live so far away. Irini came along in 1988. It's so sad that Jack never met his granddaughters but at least Maja did.. There is a lot Jack hasn't seen: electricity or running water in the house, the paved road to Kolymbithris, a telephone in the house (it took a couple of years to get used to hearing the phone ring in the house). The way we communicated when our parents were in Paros was to ring Pandelia's phone every fortnight. My parents had to walk up to the farm and wait by the telephone, the only telephone in the vicinity (another one of Pandelia's miracles).

I think, since 1969, I've missed four summers altogether. I didn't come to Paros in 1979 because, in a recalcitrant mood, we (Sabine, me and our boyfriends) decided to spend our holiday in a 2-star hotel in Cavtat, Croatia. It was fun, but definitely not more fun. In 1980 I was working to save up money to spend three months driving around the US.

In 1989 I was applying for Australian Permanent Residency and they took my passport away for eight months and in 1996 I was (at last!) pregnant with twins and both Maja and Sabine insisted that I shouldn't make the long trip and risk the pregnancy.

Paros is such a big part of our life and has such a special place in our hearts. As children Sabine and I met our soul mates that would become our husbands in Greece.
Our children have been there since they were babies and to this day it's the place where we are happiest. Whenever I arrive in Paros it's like a refocusing of the psychic map, a homecoming. I cherish the friendships that still exist, after decades. Peter first joined me in Paros in 1984 and hasn't missed many summers since. I hope Peter and I are blessed to see the next generation grow up here and the one after that. It's my second home, or maybe my first when you apply the rule that home is where the heart is. After forty-three years in Paros there are still so many corners that I need to explore. The island is so wonderfully diverse and although I have spent time each month of the year there, I hope that one day we will spend twelve months there, just for the experience. I'd love that. I'm grateful that I am able to share Paros with so many wonderful friends, locals and foreign. I am also grateful to Fionnuala and Charlotte for coming up with the idea of an e-book and making me write my memories of Paros, even though there is so much more to remember, so many more friends to mention who touched our lives.

Irene Grootendorst,
Sydney,
Australia,
 March 2012.

Florence, Desmond, Barry Flanagan and Jack Grootendorst and kids in front of the legendary ELLI.
Courtesy of Florence Tamburro

ANNELIZE'S STORY · 1972
By Annelize Goedbloed

Annelize on Paros ca 1980

Going to Paros was one of those coincidences of which one can't foresee the far reaching consequences.

It was at some New Year reception in the early days of 1972. We kissed friends and lots of unknown people with well wishes, spilled champagne and exchanged the plans and good intentions for the coming year. That is how we talked about our plan to go to Greece for our summer holidays.

' Ah', our hostess said, 'but then I have to introduce you to my friend here who has a house on an island in Greece. Perhaps he can give you some advice'. 'Yes indeed' the man said. 'I have a house on Paros, one of the Cycladic islands. Paros is the island of the famous white Parian marble. Praxiteles, statues of the Acropolis, you know. My whole house is of marble; walls, terraces, bathrooms, everything. Right on the seaside, a small private beach, incredibly clean and clear water. I have been on the island for ten years now. Naoussa is the village I refer to. With small children it is perhaps best to rent an apartment. I know everybody in the village and I could arrange that for you'. 'Wonderful. Good idea. Paros, why not?'

And that is how we found ourselves in Naoussa that summer. It had taken some serious effort to get there. First the challenge of confrontation with Athens, that hysterical, constantly shrieking wife of a city. Then the challenge of confrontation with the transportation to the island; seven slow hours on an old crummy ferryboat, people strewn all over the decks, the toilets indicated by their smell, the noise and the mess.

Naoussa was a revelation. An unpolished gem. Clichés are gluing to my fingers when I want to describe it but let me just use one; its dazzling whitewashed houses glisten against the blue sky and reflect in the clear blue sea. The maze of its narrow streets leads you from one picturesque courtyard to another photogenic corner.

Koulouria freska, a boy carrying a large basket cried out every morning, passing in the alley below our balcony. Donkeys trotted through the streets, a jute sack under the tail to collect their dung, a rugged farmer whipping it gently along and loudly announcing what sorts of fruits and vegetables it carried that day. Kaikis bobbed in the small harbour. In the morning, when the fishing boats rounded the old wall of the fort at the entrance of the harbour under a cloud of shrieking seagulls, people gathered on the mooring places to buy their catch of the night. During the day, fisherman mended the nets, adroitly holding the damaged part between toes and hands. There was the smell of fish and diesel oil. Nets, baskets, barrels and fishing gear bulged out of the storage rooms all around. The kafenion in the corner served fresh fish and the little ouzeri had a permanent flow of customers downing the local *suma*, becoming more and more ebullient, their diatribe resonating against the whitewashed buildings.

We went often to the small beaches of Kolybitres where our Dutch friends had their house. The children splashed endlessly in the shallow water, climbed the smooth rocks and looked for shells. At the end of the afternoon, we had a glass of wine on their marble terrace, looking across the bay as Naoussa slowly changed her sparkling whiteness to a rich gold in the sunset.

We discovered the minute fishing harbour of Ambelas on the other side of the island facing Naxos. Ambelas was nothing but a few farms and houses that were only occupied during the summer when half of the fishermen of Naoussa moved there for the summer to be nearer to the fishing grounds. From one of them we actually got our apartment. There was a tavern on the seaside and the beach below became our favourite spot; nice for the children and nice for us because of the great snorkelling and fishing amongst the many rocks of that coastline. We befriended the owner of the tavern. He spoke English well, which was a relaxing change from the hand-and-foot conversations with the people. He had come back from Canada where he had been a stone engraver, to marry the bride his mother had chosen for him and had started the tavern with his wife cooking delicious traditional foods. The place was the favourite party spot where people from all over the island went on Saturday night to dance to the music from the jukebox, not minding the frequent breakdowns of the rickety generator that made the music come to a whining halt.

That first summer we had the most wonderful holiday and so did the children. The best thing that happened to us was that we had such a relaxed time due to the fact that the whole village of Naoussa was looking after our little blond children so that they could roam around freely without us worrying. We often lost them to find them sitting on a front door with some *yaya*, happily spooning up a *glyko*.

This was what made us decide to go back the next summer. We had never gone back twice to the same place for our holidays. It was the beginning of a forever.

Coming back the following summer, we were welcomed as old friends. That felt great. We befriended more and more people, foreigners as well as Greeks. We started to feel at home during those few weeks, a little part of a community of Paros-lovers. We even started musing about buying a piece of land for a house.

One day, drowsily sipping ouzo, prodding grilled octopus with a toothpick and looking out over the sea at the cape of Damoulis, our friend of the tavern in Ambelas said, 'you know, that piece of land up there is for sale. The farmer needs a *prika* (dowry) for his daughter and he is selling it for a good price.' I don't know why but all of sudden I blurted: 'I am going to buy it. I just want that piece of land, my piece of land.' Perhaps it came from not having any roots anywhere, being uprooted by the Japanese war, parents having lost all, never wanting property or possessions anymore.

And so it happened. Our Dutch friend helped with the paperwork and the contract through his experience and contacts and in 1974 I became the owner of a sizable piece of land on the sea with two small beaches below it. It was on a slope, traditionally defined by the stacked walls. Most of it was arable land on which the farmer cultivated wheat. There were no trees but for a few small, wind-battered cedars. A rim of herb bushes and prickly vegetation bordered the sea. The view of the island of Naxos across the sea and past it at the far pale outlines of other islands was breath-taking.

From that time onwards we started to come by car to Paros. We had a Volkswagen camping car. In Holland it served as my every- day transportation as well as an extra bedroom when we visited friends. It also took a full hockey team, which made me always the first person to call on for driving the kids to a game. But it was slow. On the highway it had a cruising speed of 90 km. and up on a hill I had to fall back in the column of trucks. The trip from Holland to Paros took five days; three to reach Ancona, two nights and one day on the ferry to Patras, another day to get to Athens and take the ferry to Paros. For the trip to Greece I also took the dog with us; our family guardian. He was to become a noticeable feature during our holidays on Paros for never leaving any family member out of sight, protecting us and particularly me as he once attacked the papas passing too closely by me. People were scared of dogs and held peculiar ideas about them. I was once scolded for having him swim with us because he would transmit flees to other swimmers. The Greeks were not particularly animal-friendly at the time and we were constantly scared that he would succumb to the charms of a local bitch because we were told that they killed free-roaming dogs with strychnine-spiked meat.

For several years we camped under the trees on the seaside at the other side of the beach from the tavern in Ambelas. A fisherman there had given us permission to use his well and outdoor loo, so we were all set. It looked a true gypsy encampment; tent, car, cattle trailer, table, stools, washing line, water buckets. Particularly the small cattle trailer that I used for the transport of my sheep back home where I managed a small farm, added to the looks. It held the trunks with our camping gear but its use as an extra bedroom for two kids never stopped to surprise people. Camping was connected with the shaggy backpackers that would settle on a tavern chair for a whole day with a salad and a beer, so people found it very unusual for the likes of us to be camping. My husband being a surgeon, we were supposed to be filthy rich and camping was therefore completely out of place. Our Greek friends took our eccentricity however in their stride, more so since my husband helped many people with medication, consultations and some much admired small surgery on the terrace tables of the tavern.

Coming from Paroikia, at the top of the hill is the farm where donkeys once trotted round and around to thresh the wheat. That is where you have the first view of the bay of Naoussa, Kolybitres ,the monastery at the far end, the flat plain of Kamares, the windmill. Every year we all cried and clapped in joy when we crossed that hill. Leaving the asphalt road from Naoussa to Lefkes we veered off to the left on the bumpy dirt road to Ambelas. We then hastily put up camp under our familiar trees, embraced our host the fisherman and rushed down to the beach for our first swim.

Days passed lazily, snorkelling, fishing, fooling around on the beach with the children or reading under our big cedar tree with the cacophony of cicadas and often ended with long nights in the taverna, drinking, dancing the ballos, kalamatiano and sirtaki. The youngest daughter spent many a night sleeping on three chairs, only to wake up to help clean the terrace. Wobbling back to our camp over the beach with the four kids, the dog trotting ahead, glow-flies in the bushes, the sea lapping against the rocks, bush rats scuffling in the reeds, cockroaches shining in the torchlight in our borrowed loo, we had yet another short night of sleep; the sun would soon rise and the heat drive us out of our sleeping quarters.

We ventured around the island, explored other beaches, collected herbs, went on walks through the hills and admired the diversity of the countryside. Often we were invited by people to come to their house and share a glass of homemade wine "*choris pharmaka*" (without chemicals) which certainly strengthened our stomach lining. And we looked at Damoulis and made plans for the building of the house. It should blend into the countryside, look like a farmhouse that had always been there.

It took a few years to get the finances. We had already befriended the architect, one with experience on the island and great respect for the traditional Cycladic architecture. Our friend from the tavern was to supervise the construction. In 1978 we started, blissfully unaware that having a holiday house meant the end of real holidays.

The house was built in the marble stone of the island. As much went underneath to make it earthquake proof as above the ground. Building materials came by *kaiki* and were dumped on the quay of the harbour of Naoussa. Building in stone or marble had the same price, but with little knowledge of brick building and insulation, stone was the natural choice.

The building of the house went uneventfully and smoothly – except that the water tower was forgotten by the stone workers (they couldn't read the drawings.. They had left for their town of Lefkes and wouldn't come back. We therefore could only have one built of brick. This meant that it could only hold a water tank of just one cubic meter of water, which is not much, even with frugal use, for a family of six. For years we struggled every two days with the water pump - dirty spark-plugs, air in the hose - to pump water up from the big terrace cistern into the measly water tank in the tower. Ambelas had no electricity so there was no question of us having electricity. It was oil and gas lamps as well as a stove and a fridge on gas bottles. The Greek plumbing was, and remains to this day, a mystery. To know the intricacies of the piping network it is best to use a divining rod. It also forces us to impose the much loathed basket for the disposal of toilet paper.

From our house on cape Damoulis we now looked down on Ambelas and at the big old cedar trees on the seaside that was our campsite and which were the inspiration for Desmond O'Grady's poem that he offered us when we moved into the house.

THE OLIVE AT AMBILAS

By Desmond O'Grady

I've a fisherman's hut here;
halfdoor on a covered terrace,
fisherboats by sea's edge where
we swam that first year, ate
later under that great olive
one thousand years old,
olive of olives:
trunk a wrestler's torso
branches, arms of old men-
sailor, farmer, shipwright-
dancing, arms outstretched,
slow in their grace turn, heel
and toe - figures
on an ancient vase
Whitewashed my room's hermitage,
'dark by night when I shut that top
halfdoor battled with batwing thoughts
in this brain's belfry before sleep....

Desmond O'Grady, a reputed Irish poet, was a well-known figure in the group of artists that flocked to Paros for his ebullience and his wonderful readings. He wrote "The olive at Ambilas" in 1979 spontaneously when visiting my house, on a large sheet of watercolour paper, half drunk, sentences crookedly aligned, not all easily legible. I have it hanging, framed as a picture, in my living room in Delft. I recently saw him again in his favourite watering hole in Kinsale (Ireland), where he is the poet-in-residence. He has some seventeen volumes of poetry to his credit and is a founder of the European Community of Writers. He had suffered a stroke, was frail but – as during all his life - assisted by a caring lady. I learned he is in a nursing home now.

Perhaps this is the first time this poem of the "Olive at Ambilas" is published. I copied his wording with great care having to use a magnifying glass at some places where his handwriting had gone into a scrawl.

In 1979 we stayed for the first time in our house. Indeed the end of lazy holidays. We started collecting hundreds of cement bags from all around and cleaned up the terrain. I toiled around breaking my back, with heavy wheelbarrows of earth or gas bottles or stones. In early spring I came back with a full carload of stuff for the house, then in winter with friends to plant what I had bought from the nurseries in Athens, skidding in the mud from the dirt road to Ambelas and Damoulis. To make a garden with anything else than olives, wine or fruit trees – all of which don't do well in the full exposure to the North wind of Damoulis - that were available on the island, was a big problem. At that time there were no nurseries on Paros; now there are five. To this day finding the proper plant species that resist the salty sea wind remains a challenge of trial and error. We always carried loads of stuff from Holland by plane as well as on top of the car. Many simple, practical things we couldn't get on the island such as aluminium foil. Many things had to be collected from Athens. In Athens you were (and are) an absolute hero when you managed two errands in a day. One would buy a fridge, for example, pay for it, a scribble on a piece of paper torn from a newspaper being your receipt; and from that moment on it was all your problem to get it to its destination. You had to find a small truck somewhere; you yourself had to take care of the transportation from the dealer in Athens to the transportation company somewhere in Athens or Piraeus, which would then take care of forwarding your purchase to Paros. And lo and behold, your fridge would miraculously arrive in a warehouse in Paroikia. You would indicate which object was yours and go and find another small truck with a driver who was willing to go on the dirt road up to Damoulis – a task which taxis refused to do.

Having a house ties you down, you just don't seem to move away from it; there is always something that needs repair or improvement. Standing on my windy hill, looking at the black, blue and pink shadows of its mountains I think Naxos is perfectly all right over there across the sea. It took therefore years before I visited Naxos. I am just fully content with the view of it. The sky is blue Formica. Without nuances. The summer light is as harsh as the vegetation is hard and scratches my skin when I walk down to the little beach below the house. A gliding seagull shows the way, beak and wings cut out against the blue. It seems eternal. It is so quiet, so still, you can hear someone sneeze in Ambelas, you can hear the ferryboat going to Naxos before you see it rounding the corner of the island at Filisi, you can hear the shepherd up in the hills of Ysterni shouting at his sheep. It is not so much a life as an existence.

Morning
Roused by men's crosstalk
Netmending, I open halfdoor,
While light dazzles as childhood's
Image of the Devine Vision
The olive of Ambilas in the flat glare.
Exhausted by nightmare
I step over piled nets.
Here is my space; whitewashed
Stone cottages, bright boats, sea
Yet the squeeze and release of anxiety.

It is beautiful beyond words. It is also the snug self-containment that the view gives; that the rest of the world is far away and unnecessary, which is something you come to appreciate very much when you are on Paros. In fact, one descends on Paros. Whether by boat or airplane, the sensation is the same. It is like coming to another order of being. The pace of life, the quietness, the perfume exuded by herbs in the fields. My sense of distance shrinks on an island. Going from Damoulis to Aliki feels the same as going from Amsterdam to Paris. You don't do that every day either. I threaten to become a hermit. Prolonged solitary affects people in a different way. It is after all an unnatural business to find myself on an island with an under-utilized brain. Eventually it makes me perhaps go a little crazy. But then indeed you find lots of "special" people on Paros.

Because of its remoteness from public services we had no access to electricity or water. Up to this day we use the rainwater from the cisterns. You don't realize the value of electricity until you don't have it. It was the hassle with the water pumps that made me look into the possibilities to generate electricity; city electricity, windmill, generator, sun energy.

Electricity had at last come to Ambelas. It would take some thirty poles to reach me, an outrageous cost, and above all, involving the much feared labyrinth of paperwork by the "officials". A windmill is ugly, and makes noise. A generator makes a lot of noise and as a mechanical thing can break down and I didn't want to depend on anybody for repairs. That left sun energy. I asked around in Athens. Sun energy for water panels? No, for electricity. I was looked at as if I was an alien.

I brought the whole sun energy system from Holland, including the electrician to install it. He had to put all the wiring in the whole house because there was absolutely nothing. He caused such confusion in the kafenion when he asked which colour wires were used for the positive and earth etc. that he resolved to open a socket himself with his ever-present screwdriver only to find that the wires were all the same colour. We also got to know all the hardware stores and electricians of the island when searching for certain screws and bolts. It was a memorable and well celebrated moment when the first lamp was lit. That was in 1989.

The stove and fridge had to remain on gas but the pumps and lights worked on the sun energy. Now electricity is everywhere, poles and wires interfering with once pristine views. When the old gas-fridge broke down and it was almost impossible to replace it I gave in at last and I now have one pole on my land. The kitchen is now on electricity and that saves me from dragging butagas bottles. Otherwise sun energy is still the main power source and the water source is still the collected winter rain.

One day we found a note under the terrace door saying; "Dear owners. You have done a beautiful job with this restoration'. I stored it carefully in the Guest Book and still glow with pride when I re-read it, particularly when I am hardly able to stand up straight after a day's toiling.

However, not everything can be preserved. Not everything is for always. Advancement can't be stopped. Paros has been discovered! It has been promoted in all sorts of holiday brochures. It is actually amazing that it took so long. The ferryboats have improved although it took some serious disasters to do that. The little shack of an airport terminal has been replaced by a respectable building with luggage screening and all, plus bigger airplanes can now land. It seems a long time since the little ramshackle piper cubs were transporting eight passengers and the people silently made signs of the cross when boarding them, looking through the cracks at the islands passing by below. They were also always late because the pilot needed to buy fresh fish in Aliki or do some other errand before take-off. No one was bothered. People waited patiently, twirling *komboloi*, chatting, staring at the sky, judging the wind for the possible bumpiness of the flight.

The soft, rolling hills and the coast are being gnawed up by so many buildings, houses, houses everywhere. At night yellow eyes stare from the black hills in even the most remote places. Water sources are being exhausted by swimming pools and lawns and water shortage is becoming a serious problem. The celebration of Easter after church is made impossible by the nuisance of firecrackers that rip the eardrums and all the souvlas are electrical.

Tourism is the big thing. It has become the main and most often the only source of income for the majority of the population of Paros, although for just the few months of its season. Farmers have stopped farming having sold their land for a lot of money. Food, drinks, supplies, Ikea orders; everything comes on the large trucks by ferry from Athens. Everywhere tastefully decorated restaurants, trendy boutiques and bars are sprouting up. Gone are the glaring neon lights and the pictures of the Swiss Alps behind the bar of a tavern.

Greece joined the European Community and some of its subsidies indeed made it to the intended purposes. There are comfortable asphalt roads replacing the dirt roads and with them we have the roar of hundreds of rented vehicles.

With the "advancement" came also services, like gardeners and caretakers for the summerhouses. And better expertise, where before everybody just declared what he was – plumber, butcher, builder or whatever - until the contrary was proven, much to the dismay and the expense of the customer.
Paros has become chic, an "in" place for the jet set.
Unfortunately, crime followed as well and we now always have to shut doors and windows when we leave the house.

Still, walking, biking, hiking, driving around Paros out of the tourist season, everything soothingly repeats itself; sleeping villages, the dogs dozing in alleys, the trees whitewashed to waist height ,, the lonesome chapel in a field with a withered wreath on the door,, a bold old olive tree standing bravely in the scorching sun, the smell of *stiffado* in the afternoon....

> *I paddle the azure sea's edge*
> *Boats bas-relived in hard light*
> *I scramble red rock, shelved*
> *Terracotta clay to our olive*
> *Gnarled, a nuncle*
> *Manhood's mythology*
> *I feel gnarled as gnomes*
> *From doubt, belief, doubt.*

There is one thing we should be aware of and never forget; that we are guests of Paros. We will always be foreigners, we are birds of passage. For the Parians even someone from Naxos is a foreigner notwithstanding that he has lived on Paros all his life

Of the people from the first moment I came to the island quite a few are still there, either visiting every year, staying for stretches of time and some have even settled. Living year-round on the island has become attractive.

There has been an ever-growing number of writers, painters, sculptors, people doing yoga or meditation and all sorts of courses and workshops. They meet, exhibit, recite and retreat.

Unfortunately, I can't yet manage to stay long enough to become a real part of the thriving foreign community of Paros. My stays are marked by my affection and connection to my spot. It is my "point de répair", just being there, unwinding, indulging in the solitude and the relativity of obligations. That is, apart from the jobs needed for maintenance (the hardware store is my delicacy shop) and the hassle it can give when my time is limited.

My children have families and come every year to Damoulis. It is their turn to fool around with their children on the beach, worry about sunburn, collect shells, fish and snorkel. It soon will be their turn to worry and pick their children up from the disco at odd hours. My short pieces of lifetime on Paros represent a sense of the mere simplicity of existence. Far from my Dutch life, I let minutes bleed into hours. It becomes important to appreciate fleeting moments and become free of unfounded belief in permanence, free of the deceptive desire for security on which we seem to build everything. I only have to look at the damaged, once biblical, view from my kitchen window and hear the noise coming from all the newly built holiday houses. Beside the noble art of achievements there is the noble art of accepting things as they are, leaving things out that are not important.

Remember? We paddled in silence....
..Ages ago... So much has changed.
Copulation. Birth. Death.
We try to live our youthful visions
Every day a fresh start.
Every night bats in the brain...
We do what we can
Not what we envision...
So cast some shade of compassion
On the merciless light of our lives...
That is not vanity.....
With small fortitude.....
That olive
Of Ambilas.

The new moon hangs for grabbing, the setting sun casts its last tired rays on Naxos. The warm wind blows through my linen trousers, bulges my shirt, dusts my glass of wine. My sunglasses dip all in soft green oil. Nothing can happen to me.

Annelize Goedbloed
Delft, the Netherlands,
April 2012

Camping under the tree in Ambelas, 1975.
Courtesy of Annelize Goedbloed

GREGORY'S STORY · 1973
By Gregorio Altamirano

Gregorio ca 1973

Paros: The Paradise of Choice.

My craving for Greece came suddenly and unexpectedly way back in high school. It was 1969. I remember passing by a classroom and hearing some strange but exciting almost oriental sounds. Strange because I had never heard music like this before, exciting because of the strong and moving sound of a clarinet enticing you to enter into dance. As I got closer I felt an immediate affinity for what turned out to be a Greek "tsamiko", a war dance from Macedonia. As I looked into the classroom I saw what would become the catalyst for the beginning of the rest of my life. There was a very good looking black young man jumping and twirling in the air holding a handkerchief in his left hand while his partner was holding the other end supporting his athletic movements. As he jumped he slapped his foot with his hand and said a loud "Opa!" When he came down he twirled on one foot while slapping the other, his partner having some difficulty holding him up. The music continued with a clarinet playing up and down the scales in what seemed some mid-eastern orgy of feeling! I was hooked.

I entered the class, asked what the music was and if I could enroll. With the answer to the affirmative I immediately became an avid Greek dancing enthusiast. I began learning to dance by attending every class without exception and after school went nearly 4-5 times a week with a group from the class to dance and listen to live Greek music at a local restaurant or "Taverna" as it's called in Greek.

I quickly became an expert Greek traditional dancer and many times the orchestra would play especially for me, refusing to stop in order to keep me dancing. As I was graduating soon, I and my then German girlfriend, Ingrid, who also was a good dancer, decided to take a trip to Greece in order to see if the Greeks really dance the way we had been taught. We also wished see this ancient country that has been used as an example by many, if not all, politicians as the country of the first democracy. As money was tight, I decided to try to teach Greek dancing in order to make enough for my trip. I managed to convince the owner of a tavern in Oakland to let me try my hand at teaching and I soon had fifteen students coming twice a week for almost a year.

Having made enough for the trip, we decided not to wait any longer and so in the fall of 1973 headed for Frankfurt, Germany where Ingrid's family resided to see them and buy an inexpensive car to travel through Europe on our way to Greece. I managed to buy a VW bus for seventy-two dollars at an auction of the German Post Office! I built a bed inside and off we went. It was one of the most beautiful trips and one of the best cars I've ever had going down the Dalmatian Coast, then along the border with Albania. The Albanian government, at that time, didn't allow anyone in or out of the county. We entered Greece through Thessaloniki. We then headed for Athens where Ingrid, who was a stewardess and had contacts all over the world including Greece, had made arrangements with some friends who provided us with lodging for a few days.

I am giving you a brief history of my arrival in Greece for reasons you will understand shortly.

Coming into Athens, however, I saw something that would remain ingrained in my memory forever. I saw a city in darkness except for the blue flashing lights of police cars speeding through empty streets and reflecting against the sides of the buildings. There was an eerie silence that pervaded the atmosphere when suddenly we heard the sounds of gunfire.

Not having a radio in the car, we couldn't know what was happening but we slowly found our way to the house of Ingrid's acquaintances. We knocked and were let in to a living room filled with very worried looking people. They were talking animatedly between themselves while some spoke on the telephone. We were informed that there had been a major demonstration against the dictatorship by the students and the general public at the Polytechnic University. Some of our hosts' children were there when they were attacked by the army with tanks and machine guns. This incident, one of many to come, would be called the "Polytechnic Uprising".

Now we understood what was happening. By coincidence, shortly before my departure, in Berkeley California where I attended school, there were anti-Vietnam war demonstrations. They were so huge that the National Guard was called in to occupy the city, placing it under Martial Law, and to pacify us demonstrators by force. There were shootings and deaths, a curfew had been declared in the city which resembled the situation we now found ourselves in this night. I have to say I felt no panic as a feeling of déjà-vu came over me, but concern for the students and unarmed civilians that would be beaten and killed that night.

On the first anniversary of the event there was a march of over a million people in which I participated, passing by the American Embassy in memory of the dead students and America's role in the killing of democracy in Greece. I cannot describe the emotion expressed in such an event,

Needless to say, my introduction to Greece was very dramatic. I found out some days later that our car was one of the last to be allowed to enter the country before the closing of the borders for some days. I became aware through discussing with our friends that this was a much politicized country of very savvy and informed people. This awareness would follow me through the years and even to the small island of Paros.

We travelled a few days later by ferry to Paros. The ferry was flat-bottomed, which means it moved very much with any wave it encountered. On this voyage it encountered many a huge wave. This made it not very pleasant as many of the passengers got very seasick and the voyage took over eight hours. The ship was called the "Elli". I had heard a lot about the perfect weather in Greece but this day it was horrible with very high winds and a very heavy downpour. It was the first time I had ever been on a ship like this and despite the lack of comfort it was very exciting.

We arrived in darkness, a few lights showing from the village of Paroikia. It was cold and still rainy though not quite as bad as during the voyage and we walked on the seafront looking for some food and a place to stay the night. We found a little café or "kafenion" run by a Greek man of upper middle age. He had a grey mustache, was wearing a Greek sailor's cap, had bright eyes and an understanding smile, his name was Dionisakis. It was quite late; there were only a few foreigners at one table and a couple of Greek fishermen at another. We asked if there was a room to rent somewhere around and were told that above the café there were two rooms for rent. This was perfect and very convenient. This cafe was to become one of my favorite places in Paros.

The room was cold and damp but a room. Before retiring for the night we were given some hors d'oeuvres or "mezze" and some ouzo, which was much welcome following such a trip. After a few of those and feeling a bit drunk and very tired we fell immediately to sleep with intentions of moving to a place that the local butcher had arranged for us the next day.

We awoke to a sun-filled room with the sound of the sea lapping against the shore. There was a smell of Greek coffee coming from below, inviting us to rise and partake, which we did readily. We entered the café where Dionisakis was making some coffee for the fishermen sitting and smoking, a favorite Greek pastime. Two of them were playing with their worry beads or "komboloïs", a short chain or string with seventeen or twenty-one beads. The first man, handsome looking but with a weathered face, held them in one hand while allowing the beads to fall one at a time while holding the end in the other hand making a nice clicking sound. The other man, a very thin and wiry type, was flipping it around his fingers in an intricate design so quickly I could hardly see it. All of this is supposed to calm the spirits or...to impress the pretty tourist girls!

Ingrid's contact, who was a butcher and who had arranged for us to rent a summer house, came after an hour or so. He was short but well-built and handsome, something he seemed to be well aware of. His English was quite good and he explained he had learned it from the hundreds of tourist girls he had seduced. Yes, he was quite into himself. He led us up a hill where there was a working windmill and then out of the village by foot to three houses that were built next to the sea. All three had slightly different but similar architecture and had large glass doors facing the sea. The view was fantastic facing the open sea and the two outstanding rock cropping called the "Portes" or doors. They were at the sea entrance to the harbor of Paroikia and often in the summer one sees the sun setting behind them, a very dramatic and unique experience. During the day this view from the house seemed like Paradise. However, by evening we began to see that there were some problems staying in a summer house on a Greek island in the winter, namely humidity and wind.

Humidity and wind are what give an ancient look to just about everything by the end of every winter. After sleeping in a bed in a house with no insulation, we had

to wring out the covers and sheets that had absorbed what seemed to be all of the water of the island. Needless to say, barbs of ice-cold of wind hit us upon leaving the room that went right to the bone. All this was after a night of "bliss", dreaming of rowing a boat in a river upstream the whole night.

Thank God for the Greek sun! It solves all problems in a moment. I took my first walk around the area, being surprised at how dry everything looked. There were fields of golden dry grass bordered by loose rock walls. The "forest" consisted of some dozens of short, tortured pine trees and many areas were just bare stone, blasted by the Aegean storms. There were many trees by the sea, mostly pine that were brown and dry on the side hit by the wind, none of which were allowed by the Gods to become very tall. Most were bent over quite dramatically, having adjusted to the conditions of being battered by the "anemos" or wind unmercifully for years. Except for the sound of the blizzard, I could only hear the sea gulls, some sheep and goats and, of course, the roosters. Then there were few people and hardly any traffic. At that time there were very few cars on the island, one of which was mine.

This was very different from what I was used to having lived in a city all my life and just coming from Athens which was full of dramatic and noisy events. This was something very important because it leads to an understanding of the island people's psyche, their calmness and slow ways of moving and their attitude of tomorrow or "avrio" always being another day. It was something hard to get used to at first but grew on me quickly. This peace and quiet became a necessity after some time and living afterwards in a noisy city became difficult.

Time passed quickly and friends were made easily. In fact, meeting someone the first time you almost always became a friend immediately. There was no waiting period as in the States or in Northern Europe, no testing of friendship or being timid about inviting someone to dinner. Those first weeks in Paros we spent at the café or restaurant, the beach or reading at home and in the evenings partying with some people somewhere. There were no plans made, ever. Things just happened as they happened and it was good that way. There was one other very interesting thing I noticed; all doors were left unlocked everywhere! There was no crime in Greece in those years except when someone might steal a broom or some clothes, in which case it would be written off as something someone needed very badly. This made living on the island ideal because you could spend your time on important things like going to the little grocery down the way or drinking a coffee in a café by the sea without thinking of someone breaking in to your house and stealing everything. Would that this were true today as well...

After a few months Ingrid and I broke up and I found some work at a jewelry shop run by the "intellectual" of the village whose name was/is Nikos. There I met some people I would know for the next nearly forty years, most having a lot of hair, looking tanned, youthful and energetic. I got introduced to an elderly woman, an exception to the rule and former New York journalist who knew Greek. After speaking with her for five minutes I asked her if she would take me on as her student of the Hellenic language. She agreed with no hesitation and so began a long friendship, my first on the island.

After a few lessons it became clear that I seemed to have some talent for the language and progressed quickly. I am a bit embarrassed to say that our lessons consisted of conversation in Greek for about twenty minutes, a bit of grammar and then two hours of discussing about anything and everything in English. Louisa was her name and she was to introduce me to many people on the island. There weren't too many during the winter as many took off as sailors, some to Athens, but there were the permanent jobs of construction, farming, fishing, of course, running shops and the like to keep most around.

Paros actually was one of the few islands of the Cycladic area that retained its young people. Many of the islands had lost their impatient youth to the cities to be educated at university or to find non-traditional occupations as the old way of living was slowly but surely dying. However, Paros had a fledgling tourist trade, which brought many interesting people from all over the world, most of whom fell in love with the island and would come for months at a time. This created a lucrative and interesting environment for young people to open new businesses which, after a few months of hard work during the summer would provide economically for the rest of the year with some left over. Also, the charm of the island created groups of interesting and crazy people that would remain friends for many years and who would come year after year to stay and even work through the long summers. Everything was very cheap by American standards during those years and one could survive very easily on a few dollars a day. A few of these people were even relatively wealthy.

We were all in our early twenties during a time of revolution throughout the western world. In Greece the dictatorship was falling and the Vietnam War was coming to its infamous end. It was a time where young people were finding many ways of expressing themselves and had the freedom and the gall to do so. Paros was the perfect place to express one's self and to interact with others.

In the late spring of 1974 I went with a group of friends to a restaurant, "taverna" named "Damianos" which was by the sea in an area , not quite a village, called Ambelas. It was a beautiful night, calm with a full moon rising from behind the island of Naxos, huge and red, reflecting off of the sea in front of us. The place was full with Greek island music playing full blast and people already dancing. My friends immediately saw I could hardly keep still and I asked one girl from the "parea" or group to dance with me and I taught her a few steps.

There were tables full of food with more being passed around and the drink, mostly "retsina", being served by the pitcher around all the tables. After drinking a few glasses of that, we were all feeling very good and the dancing was erupting throughout the place. I decided to invite an attractive young woman from another table to dance with me... something that usually wasn't looked kindly upon in Greek pareas but this group of people was special. We danced and she told me her name was Katerina and she spoke Greek to me. I pretended to understand, actually managing some words with a good accent and so she wasn't able to see that I wasn't Greek for nearly half an hour! Later she would tell me that she felt something was strange but I danced so well, I couldn't be anything but Greek! She was to become my wife two years later. After that night, however, I wouldn't see her again for over a month as she left for Athens on the last ferry taking civilian passengers because the next day Greece went to war with Turkey over Cyprus.

And so began the blackouts at night, the ferries only allowed to transport soldiers and only allowed to navigate with their spotlights against the shore so as not to be easy targets for Turkish planes. The Greek Mirage fighter jets began flying at full speed just a few hundred meters above our heads, flying low so as not to be picked up by radar. It was an eerie time of endless political discussions among the extremely politicized Greeks, many of whose friends were in the army at that time and had been mobilized. There was a determination about those young people to get through whatever might be coming as well as keeping their humor and sarcasm about how hopeless they felt the Greek army was at that time. There were the rumors of successes however, that the Greeks had forced the Turks to retreat and then the realization that victory was turning to defeat as the Americans, the supporters of the military junta in Greece, had ordered their pawns, the colonels to order a retreat, allowing the Turks to take over a third of Cyprus which it occupies until today.

However, with this treachery came a surprise, the fall of the dictatorship. Unable to retain power after such a defeat, the dictatorship fell and Constantinos Karamanlis, a former conservative Prime Minister in the 60s, returned from exile in Paris to become the first democratic president after the '67 coup. And then began a dramatic change throughout the country.

Of course there were celebrations but more than that there was a feeling of release and the beginnings of a freedom of expression that lasted for many years after. In Paros we experienced this first-hand in that there were explosions of artistic and cultural activity as well as crazy social goings-on. I remember that after Katerina returned from Athens, having witnessed the coming of Karamanlis and his first speech in Syntagma Square, we cemented our relationship and I began my new occupation as a jeweler in the shop where she was a partner with an eccentric, royalist architect named Petros Metaxas. The shop was called the Labyrinth and was on the picturesque little harbor of Naoussa. This shop, one of the first touristic shops of its kind, became a gathering place for both foreigners and Greeks alike.

In the mornings there would be coffee in the corner with a window facing the harbor inside the shop or outside on the little veranda which was facing the fishing boats or "kaïkia" that filled the little harbor. There we would witness the drying of the fishing nets as well as the fishermen repairing them after a long night out on the sea. There was the shop across the way where Captain Yannis' wife Costanza knitted sweaters with the speed of light; so fast you could hardly see her hands as they were merely a blur. There was the large cargo boat of Captain Leonardo, a tall regal man with a large moustache who walked barefoot around the harbor with a pigeon on his shoulder. There was the little ouzeri where Dimosthenis, the proprietor would prepare octopus on his little grill and serve suma, a type of Greek grappa, ouzo and wine in the evening and Greek coffee during the morning hours. He would also, at times, take out his clarinet and play some island music while dancing at the same time. He was a good and beautiful human being.

Many nights in the shop were spent listening to live Irish music played by newly found friends of ours. There was a kind of Irish colony across the bay from Naoussa in Kolimbithres, a place of large stones that seemed to be statues formed by the relentless wind. It was founded by a poet by the name of Desmond O'Grady who would drink like there was no tomorrow and recite poetry to a fawning audience in one of the two houses he rented, in Vigla, the restaurant that was right next to the houses, or for that matter, anywhere he happened to be. We produced theater plays which were performed in front of the shop to the people from Naoussa who would fill the little square in the little harbor with tables and chairs, enjoying the crazy show in front of them, something they found new and wonderful after years of suppression. Those are a few of the things that attracted me to that wonderful island and have kept me there for decades. This life of easy work, of much play and a total immersion into that beautiful little fishing village was as near to Paradise as one could imagine. It was the catalyst for many years of imaginative activities and the development of relationships that would withstand the passing of time, creating a society of lovers of life, of living it to the fullest and enjoying just being alive.

Gregorio Altamirano, Naoussa, Paros, April 1, 2012

ALEXANDRA'S STORY · 1974
By Alexandra Senfft

Alexandra at 14 in 1976

It was only a few months after the collapse of the Junta that my mother, my grandmother, my brother and I first came to Greece.

On arrival in Athens we visited the Acropolis. My mom Erika was wearing a rather short skirt and trendy knee-length boots, walking in front of us, followed by my always-erect granny Erla, clad in trousers. The third in the line was my own little self. I was nearly thirteen years old, my semi-long haircut typical for the 1970s, and I hated the skirt my mother had forced on me. My nine-year old brother Johann Heinrich trundled behind the three generations of women, in a grumpy mood. Sightseeing wasn't at all that we children had aspired to, but then we were too young to know what to expect anyway. Yet this visit among the ancient stones remains firmly locked in my memory. We got an idea of the history of this magnificent place, while the sweet air and the soft light stroked our senses.

Only decades later I learnt that one night in 1941, Manolis Glezos took down the Nazi flag flying high on the Acropolis, thus inspiring the Greek resistance. I guess my grandmother and mother were oblivious of this fact – and had they known it, they probably wouldn't have told me. The German past wasn't exactly an issue elaborated upon in my mother's family. Denial was more the name of the game. While we walked about the ancient temples, a photographer lurking around to take shots of tourists found easy prey in us. To get rid of this insisting man, Mom bought his rather expensive large black and white pictures. Today I am glad to have them as they document my entrée into Greece.

It was on the recommendation of our friend, *Stern* magazine reporter Joerg Andrees Elten, that we took the ferry to Paros the next day. "A very special place", he had told Mom. There is not a lot I remember about our first sojourn on the island: I was too preoccupied with my pubescent situation and with the contest I had with myself reading as many books as possible within two weeks. We stayed in "Jimmy's Bungalows", located outside of Naoussa, not far from the platia. The village was small then and if I'm not mistaken, there was only taverna "Minoa" at the bottom of the main street into Naoussa. This was where anybody seeking distraction gathered in the evenings. It was autumn, and darkness plus a slight cool breeze forced people indoors rather early. Since most guests at the taverna were male, our table became the centre of attraction: My upbeat mother, accompanied only by an elderly woman and children. Every night we ate at this place, food that I had never tasted before: simple but delicious. As a welcome gesture we had carafes of retsina sent to us from various customers: there was a lot of drinking and courting going on and frequent dancing too. I think it was Damianos from Ambelas who lifted up a table covered with plates, cutlery, bottles and glasses with his mouth, while dancing gracefully at the same time. Familiar with rock and jazz dance only, the Hasapiko was a novelty to me. I perceived the breaking glass, the expressions of passion and the air of desire hovering in the room with both fascination and alienation. Mom, hungry for attention and love, was thriving. One night, the Irish poet Desmond O'Grady appeared and eloquently stole the show. My grandmother observed the ensuing dynamics with quiet, if slightly disturbed, dignity.

By the end of this first short autumn vacation on Paros, I had devoured eleven books. From then on we kept on coming back every summer. As I grew up, the place started growing on me. At first, we always used a flat in the centre of Naoussa. I remember the great number of dolls and cushions resting on the sofa and the old-fashioned wooden beds. It seemed very homely to me and, coming from a huge city, to walk the village alone felt safe. Giorgios' and Margarita's kafenion in the inside harbour became my point of reference. Soon, my brother and I learned tavli, which was a wonderful leisure pursuit before and after beach. Rice pudding and yoghurt with honey served by Margarita with a motherly gesture was our blissful daily snack, almost a ritual. Soon we got to know many of the villagers: Anna in her wheelchair who would always have a kind word for us children when we passed her tiny cigarette shop in the harbour; "Captain Leonardo" who, with what seemed to me a sublime air, watched over matters regarding his maritime territory. Among those we met were some of the young fishermen – Nikitas, Stavros and Lazaros; Dimitris, the German-speaking barber and Christos with the garden restaurant who had studied in Munich, our former landlady Marousso and so many others. Last but not least, there was of course the architect Petros Metaxas with his creative business sense and his ability to gather all kinds of people around him.

Every day my mother, my brother and I would hop on the kaíki that brought us to the beaches of Kolymbithres. Pandelia served food in her taverna by the water. When she ran out of foodstuffs, she shouted across the bay to Naoussa: "Tomates!" or "Kremithia!" and in no time her orders were delivered. This rather unique lady had her own ways and thoroughly impressed me. If my memory doesn't fail me, the house my mother rented in the following seasons was hers. Coming from a well to-do household in Hamburg, it was exciting to wash ourselves with buckets full of water from the well and to light candles and oil lamps at night for lack of electricity. The fact that there was no telephone was troublesome, though: Each time I wanted to call my father or my grandmothers back in Germany, I had to walk to Naoussa. Then, it took hours until I finally got a line – if I got one at all,

As there weren't many foreigners on Paros yet, we soon became part of a "parea". Among them were, of course, Maja and Jack Grootendorst. I was so glad they had two daughters!

Together, we found our own ways of entertainment while the adults were partying or doing whatever adults do. Up to this day, Irene and I reminisce about that night down at the beach when we happened to meet Nikitas and the fishermen on their octopus hunt. Their lamps attracted this intelligent master of mimicry out of its shelter under the rocks and caves. In the bright moonlight we walked with these fishermen we hardly knew along the shore with yet feeling totally secure. It was an act of diverse bonding – between Irene and me, between the fishermen and us, and with the island. After what seemed hours, Irene and I started worrying about being so far away from home. We said goodbye to the quietly working fishermen and returned to the house, by now a little frightened since we had no lanterns to guide us. To our surprise and relief the adults hadn't even noticed that we had been missing. Instead of going to bed, we probably went back to the beach which we soon called "Jack's beach" (and later, after his sudden, shocking death, "Maja's").

Beaches and places in Kolymbithres started getting names: "Are you going to Bamboo or Jack's today?" we would ask in the mornings as if we were fondly talking about good friends. Speaking of names: my mother was delighted to be called by her middle name Nora now, rather than by the very German-sounding name Erika which she disliked. My brother wasn't called Heiner (from Heinrich) anymore, because it was difficult to pronounce, but by his first name Johann. Only I remained Alexandra as it happens to be a Greek name – although my parents certainly did not have Paros in mind when I was born.

With the growing tourism, the island soon attracted a fast increasing number of visitors. Particularly the Irish had taken a liking to it and some enriched our growing circle with music and – of course! – alcohol. We would usually gather in "Vigla's" in Kolymbithres, a taverna run by Christos and Panagiota. Jerry from Limerick, who with his wavy golden hair looked like a bard from the Middle Ages, used every opportunity to sing melancholic or rebellious Irish songs with his big nose wobbling. He was strumming the guitar and we would join in. "I wish I was in Carrickfergus", a sad love song, was one of my favourites. "Only our rivers run free" and "Whiskey in the jar" were other part of our repertoire. Jerry's younger brother Patrick, who used to create simple but lovely jewellery, also knew how to sing, and he occasionally wrote lyrics in my notebook, adding the chords so that I could practise them. Brian was another to play his mandolin for us; his hair always shone like silver except when it was wet because he'd again fallen into the harbour after an excessive intake of intoxicating liquids. Full moon was the best occasion for raving parties when ouzo and retsina powerfully mixed with songs and poetry. Desmond would recite poems with great intonation and theatrical gestures and then Jerry, or whoever else happened to be there, would play a piece – if not Irish folk songs, they would be from Bob Dylan, Leonard Cohen or Neil Young. Those sessions initiated my interest in literature. And the music was a revelation! It was so different from the classical music, which, apart from the Beatles, I exclusively listened to at home. I was still very shy then and quite lonely because everybody seemed so much older than I, in spite of the fact that it was mostly only a few years. There were hardly any other teenagers around, therefore I felt somewhat lost among all those people that I considered adults. In one's teens a small difference in age can create a huge gap. But that gap would soon close and age would not mean a division anymore. Other than that, I did not sense any other divisions – nobody in those days cared if you were rich or poor and what your national, cultural or educational background was.

As I finished school in 1980, I became more independent and adventurous. In the long summers, young students from Greek universities would take a break in Paros and I used to hang out with them. The kafenion in the harbour was still the centre of sociability, but Petros Metaxas' "Labyrinthos" increasingly became an alternative in-place to gather. There were coffee and drinks served in the shop, and in the displays you could admire and buy the fine jewellery created by Katerina and Gregorio. "Labyrinthos" marked a huge change in the slowly modernizing Naoussa, leading us away from the locals to a community of regularly visiting foreigners and Greeks from the mainland. Bars began to replace the kafenions. Although the number of tourists rose considerably and business in town with them, Naoussa was still fairly quiet and very manageable. In those days we often slept on the beach, in communion with nature and unrestricted by the conventions that our families and societies had instilled in us since we were born. The stillness of the landscape, the captivating light, the caressing air, the sand and water and the simplicity of life enveloped us with warmth and a sense of security like home.

At the same time, this was the perfect setting for inevitable dramas of love, lust, competition, jealousy and sometimes even hate. In short, in Paros we felt very much alive. It gave those a home who felt lost in places that should have been their homes. It was a pool of "marginal people" and individuals, many of them creative and inspiring; and some very unstable. People did not ask about your past here, and you could live fully in the present tense without looking back or forward. But even on Paros, you can't run away from your history. Those who earnestly tried to were misled by a delusion because their past would creep back to hit them smack in the middle of their face. The generation of our parents, which had grown up so restricted and affected by the Second World War or the post-war famines, seemed particularly attracted by this island which resembled paradise. But it also seemed an invitation to occasionally lose one's boundaries. Yet the society, including the locals, took you for what you were with great generosity, tolerating what elsewhere would have been intolerable. If all things failed, there was always the fresh, beautiful sea and the sunset to serve as a consolation and an ointment for the injured soul.

In the late 70s my mother had found a plot of land in Agios Andreas. "This is too far away from the village", several people had warned her. But the future growth of Naoussa proved my mother's far-sightedness to build her house up there, not far from the monastery. In the summer of 1980 we moved into our new home on Paros, designed by architect Oceanis and realized by Giorgios Bizas. It was solidly built with thick walls, cooling the house in summer and keeping it warm in winter. My brother and I were both in boarding school and used to spend our summer vacations here, so in effect we were more on the island than in our hometown Hamburg.

In the beginning, we did not have electricity, let alone a telephone. It didn't bother us; it was part of our life here. Every day I used to walk many kilometres to Naoussa and to Kolymbithres and back home. The roads were safe as there was little traffic and for many farmers, donkeys were still a means of transportation. Farmer Giorgios with his stick was well-known for inviting schoene Fraeuleins, preferably the blonde ones, on to his ass's back and bringing them to his home where he served grapes, cheese and wine.

Of the very few people living in Agios Andreas then was the family of Christos Zoumis and his wife Maria with their five children Efthemios, Adonis, Irini, Anna and Garifalia. They became true neighbours indeed, always friendly, reliable and helpful. As the Zoumis children grew up, my brother and I became adults. The olive trees in our garden started sending down roots and producing their first fruit. In the 1980s, Greece and the Cyclades seasonally filled up with tourists, crowding "our" little Naoussa. Discotheques, bars, restaurants and boutiques sprang up like mushrooms.

On the veranda of our house in Agios Andreas we were far away from the hustle and bustle caused by the invasion of those strangers who came without guitars, voices and poems, who did not know how to dance the Hasapiko and ate crepes and burgers rather than souflaki. From our house up on the hill, we saw the starlit sky with overwhelming constellations, we smelt the rosemary in the garden, heard the barking dogs and the jingling bells of wandering goats.

At the end of each summer, departure felt like a painful farewell from the cradle of sensuality back to the roughness of reality. Paros - the sweetest of addictions!

Alexandra Senfft
Hofstetten, Bavaria
April, 201

Harbour of Ambelas, 1975.
Courtesy of Annelize Goedbloed

PATRICIA'S STORY · 1976
By Patricia Donnelly

In a house, (which I can no longer find), that was then the edge of the village of Naoussa, near the road to Santa Maria, was where I spent my first summer on Paros. Newly arrived from Boston, I decided to visit my family in Greece for a month, avoiding the American 1976 Bi-Centennial celebrations – a reprieve from the colonially clad citizens, parades, fireworks and other sundry events planned for that historic city. I was especially dreading the 4th of July performance, of the 1812, Overture to be performed by the Boston Pops on the Charles River. Late May was a good time to leave.

I came to Paros to visit my brother Jim, who not only had rented a house but also had a car - an old, dark green VW Bug, which ran for exactly one week before the engine blew on a dirt road near Ambelas. The only mechanic in the village emphatically declared it "Kaput". We were forced to abandon the idea of a private car and took buses, taxis and hitched to places outside of the village we very rarely left. The port of Parikia became the city to us and when we ventured there to meet a ferry arriving from Athens, carrying a friend or relative for a visit, we could not wait to return to Naoussa. The bus or taxi ride back to the village did not take long, maybe 15 minutes, but we always anticipated climbing the hill on the main road and the surprise of the turquoise sea, view of the barren tan mountains across the bay to Kolymbithres, the church on the little island gleaming white in the sun, which all overtook your visual sense. I still look forward to that view even today.

My goateed, sandy-haired, eye-glassed, six foot tall brother Jim was a jeweler and was also buying semi-precious stones and beads during his travels to India. He sold them to Greek jewelers, which is why he was on Paros. Katerina and Gregori were his friends and business associates. They were creating jewelry for and managing the big stone shop, in the Venetian harbor in Naoussa, rented by Petros Metaxas, called Labyrinthos. They would purchase not only his stones and beads, but also the jewelry he created from them-mostly earrings and necklaces of carefully strung stones, silver beads and wire.

Kat and Greg were the first communists I ever met. Their generosity, hospitality, and openness stunned my American sensibilities. How could these nice people have caused the black listings of the McCarthy Era not too long ago alive and well in the States? Was my government really afraid of Katerina and Gregori? As I got to know Kat, I was moved by the stories of Greece during WW II and the civil war. Stories of family imprisonment, torture under the Junta, the starvation of the Greek people under German occupation-it was an eye opener for me.

It was also the summer of the Irish. They had taken over a part of Kolymbithres and came across the bay every night and invaded this small Greek village with mandolins, guitars and poetry. With almost complete abandon, we would all gather nightly at the café in the little Venetian port, owned by Jorgo, Margarita and Christos. When Jorgo, Christos, and Margarita could stay no longer they would lock the doors of their café, place a bottle of something good to drink on our outside table and wearily but with great amusement say good night and leave our group to continue on- which we did.

In the midst of the Irish summer arrived Callie, a 120lb pure black Belgian Shepherd. Callie was dropped off by a friend in the throes of her own Greek Drama. "Just for a few days," she said. So, into the three- roomed house Jim had rented, amongst visiting family, lovers, various friends coming and going, moved Callie. A month later, Callie had become quite accustomed to daily life on Paros. There were the daily swims and marathon sun bathing on a deserted beach called Santa Maria. There were few houses there and even fewer people. Most days we had the beach to ourselves. Callie loved the water and out for a swim you could grab hold of her neck and she would pull you around for as long as you liked, swim you back to shore and jump back in to the sea to accommodate the next swimmer. She did this for the hours we stayed on the pure white sand beach, and I mean hours. We would arrive in the morning and not leave until late afternoon. I was perplexed by the fact the Greeks would arrive for their beach time when we were leaving, always in hats and covered up. At the time I did not know how smart they were. A friend of mine, years later, told me when he was a young boy his father took him on their fishing boat to Mykonos. As they were approaching the shore, he asked his father why he had taken him to see all the dead bodies lying on the beach. His father laughed and told him they were foreigners taking the sun. He was completely confused by this concept of getting a suntan.

After the beach we would sometimes walk to the village, with Callie, for a dish of Margarita's rice pudding and a coffee. Most times, since she makes the very best rice pudding, it was all sold. We would then wander to the yogurt shop, in the middle of the village, to see if we could buy a bowl of freshly made yogurt. Often, he was closed because the village was too busy and had gone home. The next stop would be the café in the square-we would sit under the big eucalyptus tree and sip a Nescafe, the only coffee available besides Greek coffee. There the tavli games were in full swing, gossip and political ideas we couldn't understand exchanged, and children would be running, playing in the streets without fear of traffic because there was none. There were only a few cars in the village and trucks that would deliver produce, the buses, and, if I remember correctly, two taxis. Once in a while, there would be a beer shortage because the boat carrying the beer had bypassed Paros or the winds prevented the boat from leaving Athens. When the beer delivery truck arrived, after a few days of no beer, there would be applause.

As we dressed in the evening for our epic nights of wine, food, poetry and song, Callie would run and get her leash and sit patiently holding it in her mouth until we clipped it onto her collar. She would guide us through the narrow whitewashed streets, as children and adults alike would scatter from us crying "Lykos Lykos". (Wolf, Wolf) The Parians, at the time, had a great fear of dogs and rabies. The few dogs that were on the island were hunting dogs. They lived in country places like Ambelas, and Santa Maria and were very rarely seen in the village. Hence the panic when Callie appeared in the evenings.

Most nights we would all meet at the Labyrinthos. We would sit on the low stonewall of the shop and face the Venetian Port of Naoussa, which housed the fishing fleet. Drinking our ouzo or beer, nibbling on mezzes, we would sit and watch the fishing boats bob as if they were toys. Sometimes we would play tavli. These games often turned into a lengthy affair that would last for hours. After dark, sometimes the clarinet would appear in the ouzeria next door and the Greek dancing would begin. People would hear the first notes and be on their feet. Men would dance with other men, grandsons with their grandmothers, young girls with their uncles, husbands with their wives, neighbor with neighbor. I was always asked to join the circle. My clumsy attempts at dancing were appreciated. The Greeks would pat me on the back and say "Bravo." If the winds were up, we would move into the shop. Kat would have Bob Dylan on the tape deck and we would entertain the potential customers who actually had the courage to enter the shop with us all there. Many times they would sit and join us for a while.

Around midnight we would head out to one of the three restaurants in the village for dinner. Most nights it was LeJerrys, then across the bridge, for our meal. From there we would head to Jorgos and Margarita's cafe in the little port where the mandolins would appear, guitars would be strummed, poetry recited and songs would be sung by a group of unlikely friends, relatives, and new arrivals who would ease into the morning hours. Most times we were the only non-Greeks at the port.

On the few nights I was home before sunrise, I would get up just before first light and head to the café in the little port for coffee with our visiting dog. I would sit and watch the fishermen mend their nets, prepare their boats for fishing trips, watch shopkeepers washing the street and the entrance to their shops and listen to the banter of the beginning day.

When Capitano Leonardo was there he would join me. He was head fisherman, a robust and ageless presence that dominated the port at the time. He would sit unperturbed by the black lykos at my feet. Callie was more interested in any crumbs left from the night before than she was in startling the man sitting across from me. We would sit sipping coffee, my two words of Greek having been spoken and watch the day begin.

Callie left us in mid-August to return to her home in Athens. We were very sorry to see her go. She was a great dog and after she left the villagers would ask "Pou ine lykos?" (Where is the wolf?)

Needless to say, my stay was extended and I did not return to the States for two years. My time was not all spent on Paros then, but I have returned to build a house in Damoulis with my sister Rosemary. My brother Jim's son Luke is a frequent visitor, my sister's children Anthea and Alexi try not to miss a New Year's Eve and part of their August vacations on the island. They have developed their own bond with Paros, as have many of their friends who have spent time at our house.

The cast of characters has changed, families have grown, tragedies survived. joys embraced but that summer of abandon, surrounded by the sea and stark landscape of barren tan hills, forming unique and lasting "parea"(company of friends), grounded me with a sense of zoe (life). I think this is the common bond of the company of friends now present on Paros. I often wonder what is it really that draws me back to this familiar yet foreign place, this island that at times completely baffles me, frustrates me with a logic that exists nowhere else in the world, creates drama where no drama should exist, opens it heart with intensity to a foreign community, yet we will never completely understand the island, and I have concluded it is all these things.

When I first came to Paros I stood at the back railing of the chugging ferry, watching Parikia come into view, with strains of Greeks, young and old, singing Theodorakis songs on the deck, yayas, dressed all in black, bustling to gather together their cheeses and chickens, and wondered what adventures this island had in store for me for the week I was going to stay.

Today, I stand at the back of the High Speed, watch Parikia come into view, now very familiar, with Greeks gathering together their dogs, cats, computers and other belongings, and with much the same excitement and anticipation, wonder what adventures this island, which has become my second home, has in store for me this time.

Patricia Donnelly
Olympia, Washington
January 2012

View over Ambelas, 1975.
Courtesy of Annelize Goedbloed

MARY & BERT'S STORY · 1977

By Mary Bilz & Bert Jones

Mary and I came to Paros pretty much by chance. In the fall of 1977 we decided to empty our savings account and take some substantial time off from working. We would fulfil our sketchy dream of living on a Greek island. We took a Freddie Laker flight from New York to London and after a day or so there we bought tickets on the Magic Bus to Athens.

The bus trip itself was exciting and a little stressful. The drivers were Greek and apparently desperate to get back home. As the bus barrelled down the highway with bouzouki music blaring from the speakers, the one currently driving pantomed extreme sleepiness and fatigue. Without stopping or slowing down, he jumped out of the driver's seat into the aisle while his partner leapfrogged over the back of the seat and grabbed the steering wheel. After two days travel, including passport unpleasantness in Yugoslavia, we were dropped off in grimy Omonia Square late at night. We found an unattractive hotel and by the next day were having second thoughts about Greece as a relaxing interesting place to visit.

But we went to Piraeus and bought tickets to Paros pretty much by chance; it was the closest island that we had heard anything about. Late that afternoon we were sitting in a café in Paroikia on the paraleia having a cold beer and admiring the sunset. What a relief. The owner of the café put us on to a room that was lovely and had an ancient column drum built into the marble wall above the bed. I don't recall what we had for dinner but between the friendly people and the sunset and the couples walking along the shore in the evening we were hooked.

We met people from the Art school and some of the resident expats. Alda and Lois were two retired American women who we met and who provided us with introductions and invaluable information about rental houses and good places to eat. So we decided to stay in Paros for a while and found a little house to rent that overlooked the port and was in the middle of a bunch of small farms. It was a couple of miles from town at the foot of the mountain below the big abandoned monastery that you can see from the port.

 We soon settled into the relaxed tempo of island living. Paros was full of interesting people from all over the world. We met the Brennans and their two lovely little girls. Rory introduced me to his countryman Desmond who lived in Naoussa. He too was a poet and a well-known translator who somehow managed to get a tremendous amount of literary work done despite an unquenchable fondness for drink.

Up on the hill where we lived we met and got to know our neighbors. They were all farmers. They considered us quite a curiosity but they were friendly and encouraged our efforts to learn Greek. We bought eggs and various edibles like home-made cheese from our landlord Panayiotis' wife Anna, his mother and others.

Everyone farmed and no tiny corner of land was left untended. In front of our house, where an American house would have a lawn, Panayiotis grew grapes. The grandfather wore a knitted *fanella* under his old wool suit coat in all weather conditions and was an energetic farmer. He plowed and cultivated his olive trees and vines with a donkey. The "fields" he worked were narrow terraces, *pezoulakia* that ran up a steep hillside. When he finished with one he'd load the old wooden plow on the donkey's back and with an amazing repertoire of whistles, kissing noises and buzzing fart sounds persuade the donkey to climb the retaining wall to the next terrace. We saw old ladies in the fields bent over double prising dandelions out of the rocks with old table knives. No matter how many they gathered, more sprouted and bloomed all around our little house.

That year's wheat harvest was unforgettable. The landlord and all his cousins and friends drove donkeys loaded with sheaves of wheat down the narrow path between our front wall and the landlord's walls and unloaded all the grain in a circle about ten meters in diameter with a post in the center. A horse was attached to the post somehow and led in a circle to trample the grain and people tossed the trampled grain stalks in the air with pitchforks. That's how they threshed their wheat. It could have been a painting by Breughel or, more to the point, a scene from the Iliad. I felt incredibly privileged to observe people practicing ancient agricultural techniques. People on Paros had been threshing their grain that same way for thousands of years. It was stimulating to get into those ancient rhythms. I got the feeling that we had stepped back in time to a more humane civilized era. At that time, back in the US people were trying to come to grips with the just finished, seemingly interminable war in Viet Nam that had pitted a modern mechanized society against an ancient agrarian one. Like a lot of people, I was conflicted over the benefits of so-called scientific advance; chemicals in the food and rigid social organization.

In Paros our landlord Panayiotis was the only person we knew who owned a car and he seldom drove it. When Spiros or other neighbors went to church they hitched a wagon to a two-wheeled "rototiller" type tractor and with the man of the house sitting in the front of the wagon holding the handlebars, the rest of the family perched around the perimeter of the wagon and bounced along the rutted dirt roads to town. We became friends with some our neighbors. There was a wonderful family that lived along our route to town. Spiros was a hardworking farmer. He and his wife Maria worked harder than anyone I ever knew. They had a son, Athenasis, who was about four years old and a beautiful blonde daughter named Theodoulia who was eight or nine. Mary and Maria hit it off. We practiced our Greek with them and they showed us how they basically grew everything they ate and made everything they used. Mary helped them crush grapes for wine. When we had dinner at their house we ate cheese and olives and olive oil and hortas and bread and whatever meat, chicken, or lamb – everything from their little farm. I think Maria made most of the family's clothes. She was from Ioannina and I think she missed her family and the mountains of northern Greece.

The islanders were genuinely interested in eating pure food and drinking pure water. When someone offered you wine or olive oil he had made he always said "Ohi farmako" meaning without chemicals, and many of our neighbors took long walks with pack animals to special springs they knew where they thought the water was particularly pure.

Social life on Paros revolved around the cafes. We learned that there were several good places to hang out and drink and meet other expats and, for that matter, local Greeks. Just about everyone spent time in the cafes and pastry shops. The Port Café was especially popular whenever a ferry was due. We sat and had beer or coffee –depending on the time of day - at metal tables under the awning. There was always octopus drying on the metal pipes that supported the awning. In the evenings the two brothers that ran the place grilled the octopus tentacles and served little slices with shots of ouzo. Every day when a ferry was scheduled to arrive the place would fill up with people either to meet someone coming in or to go to Athens or another island. But a lot of us were there just to observe the action and see who might be getting off the boat. The crowd grew larger as the scheduled arrival drew near and excitement peaked when the boat was spotted rounding the point when they always blew the horn. The pier would be jammed. There were people with hand carts loaded with merchandise and luggage to be loaded on the ferry, trucks waiting in line to go on board, the officious port police and various characters trying to inveigle newcomers to stay at their "hotels". One little character circulated around shouting "Rooms, Rooms", Rooms, Rooms" as though he was imitating a motorcycle.

The other highly- favored watering hole was Dinosakis', a short walk down the shoreline from the busier more commercial Port Café. Dinosakis' bar was an old-fashioned place with high ceilings and big windows as well as a few tables out front. Dinosakis himself was the archetypical bartender. Tall and distinguished looking, he remembered everyone, greeted them by name, remembered what they liked to drink and what they were interested in. I remember watching the Muhammad Ali, Leon Spinks rematch there. The place was packed. Ali had lost the last fight to Leon Spinks and the crowd was cheering him to avenge his defeat. He did not disappoint. Dinosakis sold a lot of beer that afternoon.

We met and became friends with Fokion who worked for the telephone company up at the microwave relay station on Profitias Elias. He seemed to spend the rest of his time at the beach or flirting with girls at the various cafes as a would-be *kamaki*. He, like us, considered himself a foreigner since he was from Lesbos, which everyone referred to as Mytilini. After we became friends, he invited me to visit him at his workstation on the mountain top. Getting there was an odyssey. First we rode in a car to the end of the road where a family had a little farm. The woman worked for the phone company too and accompanied us on the substantial walk to the station on top of the mountain. She had a donkey loaded with food and drink as well as linens and whatever else was needed at the station. We had a good dinner and Fokion showed me the station. It wasn't just for the telephone. In those low-tech days the station handled defence communications and kept Athens in contact with Crete and the rest of the far-flung Greek defence establishment. My big attraction was that after the telephone traffic died down around 2am I could call the US for free. That was a treat.

After a few months on the island I lost interest in writing -writing the great American novel had been my ostensible purpose for our spending an extended period abroad. I found a job in town as a mechanic and welder. I managed to make just enough money to pay the rent and take care of our basic necessities.

Mary energetically pursued her fascination with plants and flowers. She knew many of the neighbor women and asked them about the flowers and herbs that grew everywhere. Whenever we went anywhere she collected and photographed the local flora. She hiked around the island and found terrestrial orchids, cyclamen, anemones and poppies. She learned about the culinary herbs and herbal tisanes and she collected *tsai touvounoe, faskomilo*, thyme, rosemary and oregano as well as a hundred other plants that I never knew existed. On one of our trips to Athens we got a book on Greek flora and she used it to identify the shrubs and trees that grew along the paths we walked back and forth from the beach and to and from town.

Living on Paros was extremely cheap at that time. I can't remember how much meals at the tavernas cost but it wasn't much. The food was pretty much the same at all the places: pasticcio, moussaka, maridthes, hortas, horiatiki salads, *gigantes* beans, *avgolemono soup* and the ubiquitous pitchers of retsina from the barrel. It was heavenly. We had a favorite place where we ate frequently. It was about a half an hour walk from our house but in those days we were used to walking a few miles whenever we needed anything or for no reason at all. Occasionally we ran into a couple of brothers who owned a little freighter that delivered cement from Volos all over the Cyclades and hauled whatever cargo they could arrange to ship back up to the mainland. The name of their worn-out old ship was the Lambrini and when they hit town the tavern stayed open late. Everyone drank too much and the boys put on Greek dancing spectaculars.

The most renowned dancer in town was the *fanargis* whose name I have forgotten. He was distantly related to Ioannis Parios who was from the island and was a popular singer all over Greece at that time. The fanargis was said to be the best dancer on the island. I was more fascinated by his tin-smithing than his dancing. He was a master of making all sorts of utensils out of shiny tin sheet metal that he formed into cones and circles and crimped into rosettes. He soldered them together to make lamps for ikons, candle sconces and pitchers for olive oil, as well as half-round pails with a faucet on the bottom so someone without running water could wash their hands.

People have asked me how we could have spent so much time on such a small island but frankly I don't think we ever saw the whole place. We used to ride the bus to Lefkes. Alda's friend Lois was interested in real estate and knew of places that were for sale. One house in Lefkes could have been had for less than $1,000. Buying a house wasn't in our budget though. Our rent was $40 a month and I know we spent very little on food and groceries.

We loved and eventually lived briefly in the village of Lefkes. Our favorite café stood by the magnificent church and had beautiful olivewood tables and a view down the Byzantine road towards Marmara and across the water to Naxos. We had heard the stories from long ago when villagers on the coast fled from pirates or crusaders up that road to safety in Lefkes. When we were there in the mid-seventies Lefkes was practically uninhabited. Many of the houses were closed up. There were only a few stores and nothing much to do except drink coffee and look out the window of the café. The houses in the town were very old and beautiful. It was obvious the town had been prosperous a hundred years before since many of the houses were large and ornate.

Lefkes had the last operating windmill on the island. One day when the mill was operating I walked out and met the miller. He was a fascinating character. I think his name was Dimitri. He told me about the old days when windmills operated all over the island. The mill was a fascinating and complicated machine that was practically 100% hand-carved hardwood, gears, bearings and all the running gear. He explained to me how the gears were carved, how the millstones were rigged up into the top of the mill and how the sails could be adjusted to compensate for different strengths of wind. He had clear memories of the German occupation during WW2 and one of the sails on his windmill was made from surplus material from the war, sacks or something. It had a big black swastika stamped on it. He told me a story about one festival night when the millers were celebrating but at the same time taking advantage of the wind to make flour. One miller had too much to drink. The wind picked up but he wasn't paying attention. He should have stopped the wheel and reefed the sails but the mill ran out of control. When he realized what was happening, he applied the primitive brake with all his force but there was no stopping it. The friction of the millstone running so fast set fire to the mill and the whole thing burned down.

We became friends with an old couple we met in Lefkes: Louisa and Nikos. They were very friendly and talkative. They owned a general store and had lived on Paros in Lefkes all their lives. We understood enough Greek by that time to follow their stories about the old days on the island, how forty or fifty years before Lefkes had been a bustling prosperous town with families in all the houses. In those days, Lefkes was richer than Paroikia. Mary bought a beautiful old bedspread from Louisa embroidered out of handspun wool.

In all, we spent just over a year in Greece. We were able to travel on the mainland and to other islands as well as the Peloponnese. In retrospect, I think we were lucky to have done it when we did. Greece wasn't yet part of "Europe" and Paros was just on the verge of rampant commercial development. We were fortunate to have experienced the island and its residents at that point in time. I don't think we'll ever forget the friendly people and good times we had there.

Mary Bilz and Bert Jones, Wallingford, VT, USA. April 2012

Krios Bay seen from Krotiri headland. 1969.
Courtesy of Robin Brown

FIONNUALA'S STORY · 1977
By Fionnuala Brennan

Fionnuala with Fiona and Orla in 1978

Serendipity

Serendipity is a great thing. The best things in life are often free and they frequently happen by chance. That is how we came to Paros on a cold, windy but sunny day in November 1977. We had left a warm, sunny!!!! Ireland in September and arrived in a cold, pouring with rain, stormy Athens. There were no ferries to any island, not due to strikes, the present cause, but to gale force winds, which kept them all in the port of Piraeus for nearly a week while the Brennan family languished in a cheap hotel.

The family consisted of me, husband Rory and our two small daughters; Fiona was just two years old and her sister Orla was five. Fiona resided in a buggy, which was festooned with plastic bags containing nappies, wipes and other toddler paraphernalia. Orla carried her teddy and clothes in a small red rucksack and we parents stumbled along under enormous rucksacks and sundry cases containing everything we thought we'd need for several years on a Greek island. We did not yet know *which* Greek island, but we had certain criteria which the chosen island would have to meet, including a doctor, fresh vegetables, sandy beaches where children could build sandcastles, cheap houses to rent in villages near the beaches, and, of course, friendly people.

We tramped on rickety old ferries such as the *Elli* and on rattling old buses to and around Samos, Rodos and Kreti. All were dismissed as unsuitable for different reasons. Samos had too many soldiers. I grew up in Northern Ireland and did not wish to see any more soldiers. Rhodos was far too touristy and the villages in Kreti were all up in the mountains, far from sandy beaches. The kids were growing understandably fractious and weary of our nomadic existence; it was getting darker and colder by the day and we needed to find a home soon. Andros might be nice, or Milos. So we set off from Kreti northwards.

We stopped at Paros en route and fell in love. Simple as that. All criteria were fully met and more. The light, the dazzling Cycladic houses, the small, white, blue-domed churches dotted everywhere. Agia Paraskevi, Agios Johannis, Agios Pandelis and, of course, that magnificent church of the Panagia, the Ekatonapiliani in Paroikia, all blessing the gentle landscape and wonderful labyrinthine villages.

That is why and how we first came to Paros. I have recounted in more detail why we left Ireland with two small children to live simply on a Greek island in my book, *On a Greek Island* (1998, Poolbeg).

Paros in the late 70s was still a wonderfully unspoilt place. There were tourists, of course, but not so many as to affect the innate hospitality and friendliness of the islanders. The only tarred roads I can recall were a strip over the hill from Paroikia to Lefkes and the main roads from Paroikia to Naoussa, Aliki and Pounda. The Kamares road was dirt, as was the road to Marpissa, Drios and beyond which passed our present house in Isterni. What bliss, no traffic! No jams at Ghikas' corner as there was no periferiakos. What is now the ring road was a dirt track with one of two houses off it. Bret Taylor, the founder of the Aegean School of Fine Art, and his wife Gail, lived in one, and an older couple called Robbie and Dolo lived in another. Apostolis, a guy who appeared from time to time on the island, always clad in spotless white shirt and trousers (he worked on ships) owned land along the track. As far as I remember, there were about half a dozen taxis on the whole island. Donkeys were the main mode of transport for most farmers. We foreigners who could afford it had 50 cc *papakis* or other motorbikes. The rest used shanks mare and the walking did us all good. I only remember two people who owned that most luxurious vehicle, a car. One was the so-called Doctor Bob at Parosporos and the other was Robbie Clarke-Ames who ran Robbie's Bar at Jimmy's Bungalows in Naoussa. He had a low, brown, sports car which I once witnessed marooned in a winter flood outside the village.

The lack of cars made for a tranquil place to live and also meant that a journey to the other side of the island was a day's adventure. In winter- time the buses only ran around school times so one could get into Paroikia in the morning with the school kids and from there travel onwards to Naoussa and return at noon. I think the last buses left around four in the afternoon. The carless distances also meant that some of the foreigners on the Paroikia side did not know those from far-distant Naoussa, Drios or Lefkes. Rory and I did know people from the other side because we met an Irish poet called Desmond O' Grady who lived above Kolimbithres and through him we met Robbie and his Italian wife Marise. Their daughter Victoria played with our two girls and lent them very welcome toys and books as the poor children only had a teddy and a set of Lego to play with. There was a limit to how much we could fit into rucksacks or that a child of five could carry from Ireland.

One day I was in Paroikia doing some shopping and met Desmond who introduced me to a woman of about my age, (early 30s) who had come into town on her donkey. When she heard we had girls she exclaimed, *great, they can play with my daughter, Gaia.* They did, and we have been friends for thirty-five years since then. Phillada and her partner Gerard were among the *old timers* on the island. Phillada has her own stories to tell. Other playmates for Orla and Fiona were Jan and Roy Leithen, sons of Pauline and Dick, again Parian old-timers with their own stories to tell, and James and Charlotte Miller, Diana and Colin's children who lived near us above Parosporos. Bahadour and

Vanessa Moussa, children of Georges and Martine were a bit younger but came to birthday parties with the others.

To get to know Paros better, one day in early summer Rory and I set off to walk around the whole island, along the coast as far as possible. I will never forget the beauty of that two-day walk. The wildflowers, the wild landscapes, the beautiful old farmhouses unobtrusive on the land, the donkeys in the fields. We had our siesta on the first day in the shade of a tree at Ambelas. There was nothing there except Damianos's taverna and one or two fishermen's houses and further along on the promontory overlooking the bay was, what seemed to us, the enormous house of a Dutch couple. We walked on past Molos, Marmara, Marpissa to Drios and at nightfall found ourselves above Tripoti. There we intended to bed down for the night by the side of the road. A German couple happened along, asked what we were doing, who we were etc. There were not many *xenia* on Paros at that time so we all talked to any we met. They ended up inviting us to stay the night with them in a sea captain's house which they were renting by the sea. This was one of the very few houses between Drios and Aliki. When I pass that way these days, I am constantly astounded and somewhat dismayed by the proliferation of houses there, as well as all over the island, and sometimes I really regret the fact that the road was paved, thus allowing this unregulated building explosion. After a very convivial night with our new friends, Wolf and Barbara, we walked on next day back to our little house beside what we called Delfini Beach, now called Magaya. Our visiting friends from Ireland had kindly looked after Orla and Fiona.

Orla had already spent one year at school in Ireland and had learned to read and write as well as some Gaelige. We decided that we would home-school her in Greece and so we took it in turns to teach her. This was not easy, as I discovered that my endless patience with other people's children did not extend to our poor little daughter when it came to spelling and arithmetic. *What do you mean you can't spell that word? Your Daddy taught it to you yesterday. Of course you can add 14 and 28.*

We struggled along for a year and the following year we decided that it might be better all round if Orla attended the *demotikon* in Paroikia. She would learn Greek, make friends and get away from an impatient mother's teaching. So we went to enrol her for the next term. *Is she baptised? Yes. Orthodox? Well no, Roman Catholic.* Still, she was accepted and she and James Miller were among the first foreigners at the school and certainly were the only ones there in 1978. None of the teachers spoke English and so I had to get out my dictionary and phrase books and start improving my very basic Greek. We bought Orla's school uniform, which was a blue dress with a white collar and off she went into the *proti taxi*.

Yiati klei? The teacher said to me on the second morning. Why does she cry? *Did you cry in school, darling?* I asked her as we walked home along the road above the sea. *Yes, she said. Why? Because I don't know where to sit and when I sat in the same place as I sat yesterday some kid pushed me out and I don't know what they are saying. Do other kids cry? Yes, some of the girls.* That problem was sorted when I mentioned to her teacher that it might a good idea if the children were all given designated seats and sat there in security for the term. The teacher somewhat reluctantly agreed and peace was restored. And Orla learned Greek in double quick time so she soon understood what the other children were saying.

Our first Christmas on the island is unforgettable. There had been a bottled-gas famine for a number of weeks and the electricity supply was intermittent at best. On top of that, the weather was not kind: the wind howled from Siberia, the rain lashed against the rattling windowpanes. So there we were, without heat or light in the depths of a Greek winter. Daily, we scoured the nearby beaches for driftwood but found little. We had invited a gang of xenia for the festivities and we all huddled in our living room, using body heat to stave off hypothermia. I had baked the first Christmas pudding of my life in Ingrid's oven. She was the only person I knew who had such a luxury. She collected me and my ingredients on her bright yellow motor-bike and we hit the road for her house in Pethaloudes. Ingrid later became a Buddhist nun and her house a sanctuary or little monastery. We had a stake in that property because, as was the xenia custom of the time, we had helped to restore the old farmhouse. We went there on work brigades, spending the day cutting and stripping bamboo for the roofs, mixing cement by hand and such tasks.

When our *choma* roof leaked all over our house so that one night we had to sleep with umbrellas opened over our heads in the bed, the work brigade turned up to help to repair the mud roof. They plonked some tar solution over the cracks and that more or less lasted for another year. Our landlord had taken no responsibility whatsoever for his defective property. When we went to his house in the village to inform him about our sieve-like roof, old Nomikos smiled and said, *I have the solution .Dhen birazi*.He demonstrated this wonderful solution by putting on his hat and overcoat and climbing into his bed. *See*, he said. *Nice and warm*. No mention of wet or raindrops falling on his head. *Dhen birazi*

One of the best memories of those early days was the camaraderie and helpfulness among the foreigners. If someone had a problem, the gang would turn up to help out. We had no source of heat and two small children in a very cold winter. One day, an American we called Alaskan Peter, a neighbour from up the road near Parosporus, dropped by and saw our situation.

That afternoon he delivered a paraffin heater for us to use. Our children referred to him from then on as Peter Heater. We would sometimes visit him when we were out rambling around and he would always produce bread and honey for the kids and a glass or three of rich, red farmers' wine for us. Peter had a brother called Paul who later on helped us to restore the old bakery at our house in Isterni.

In the middle of Paroikia lived two wonderful American ladies who were a good deal older than the rest of us (we were all fairly impoverished dropouts of one sort or another in our late twenties or early thirties). Alda and Lois were substitute mothers to many of us. They had what you could call soireès in their house, which was always open for visitors. They lent us books and cooked us meals. Lois was the younger and was a great work- brigade organiser. So and so has a leaky roof, she'd tell us and the next thing we'd be on the bus to Lefkes clutching hammers and shovels for a day's work on Lefkes Claus's house.

Louisa also lived in Paroikia in the house next to what is now the back door of the Aegean Centre. She had a PIANO and regular copies of *The New Yorker* and was always good for an acerbic discussion on the affairs of the world. Nikos Saris was a friend of hers and played the piano there. I don't know what happened to that piano when she died. It may be the one in which is now in the Archilikos hall. Susan James, a very good friend of ours, was a young English woman not long out of university, who had come to Paros in 1978 (and who has lived here since) very kindly looked after Louisa when she was old and very ill.

Another older and much loved resident, also now sadly deceased, was Gretchen, another American. She lived in a perfect little doll's house in one of the back streets of the village. (I think the house is now used as Jane Pack's studio) She was always gracious and welcoming to anyone who dropped in to visit. Most of us lived a fairly basic, rough and ready life, and it was therefore such a treat to be invited to dinner with Gretchen. She served a delicious meal on china plates. We used silver cutlery and drank from crystal glasses with linen napkins on our knees. Civilised luxury!

Our next-door neighbours were Elias and Maria and their children. They were farmers and we bought our milk, eggs and vegetables from them. Every morning, long before we were compos mentis, their daughter Eleni, a teenage nymph with the classical features of a beauty from a Greek vase, would ride up to our house on her donkey, bringing us our daily litre of milk. Some mornings, instead of leaving the milk on the doorstep, Eleni would venture unannounced into our bedroom to wake us up. I suspected that she was also interested in what might be going on there.

Maria taught me how to card and spin wool. We used a wooden spindle of a type used in biblical times. It is not easy to spin wool from a tangled mass of greasy sheep's or goat's wool. Maria, of course, did it with ease and produced perfect, non-lumpy yarn. She laughed at my efforts which nearly always resulted in a dropped spindle, broken yarn or, at best, a length of bumpy, lumpy wool. I persevered and managed finally to produce fairly passable wool. Next came dyeing and weaving my precious yarn.

Another American friend, Mary Bilz, (come to think of it, it seems most of the xenia in those days were from the US of A) knew about natural dyeing, so she and I went on expeditions into the hills searching for natural dyes. Phillada taught me how to weave, first on a back-strap loom like those used by Indians in Latin America, and later on her big floor loom in her house in Kamares. I would buy the fleece from Elias, wash it in the sea, card it to remove tangles, twigs and other debris, spin it into yarn, then dye it, and finally weave my wonderful creations. I wove bags, seascapes, abstract designs, and finally progressed to garment manufacture. I proudly wove a waistcoat for Rory in tones of brown, gray and white. He wore it once and declared that he had almost fainted with the heat of it. *It's like wearing a carpet*, he said. I still have that *carpet* in a bottom drawer so if a new ice age comes upon us, he will not freeze.

So you see, I was kept busy. There was my creative wool work, teaching Orla, looking after Fiona, learning Greek, writing short stories, and also doing my share of household chores. We had intermittent electricity, no bathroom, no running water in our one-bed roomed house. So we had to heat water on a gas ring (if we were lucky enough to have a gas bottle with some gas in it) and bathe the children in a large plastic tub in the living room. The clothes were washed in a well in the field nearby, not in the well, of course, in a basin of well water. On windy, cold, winter days this was not the most pleasant of occupations but on sunny days, when one could pause to listen to the birds or admire the blossoms on the trees, and the wild flowers in the field, the outdoor laundry was almost a pleasure.

After a few months on the island, it leaked out that Rory and I were experienced language teachers and we were asked to give English lessons. I took on about half a dozen students. (Rory was too busy writing his first book of poems, *The Sea on Fire*, which was published the following year and won a major literary prize in Ireland.) Among my students was a lovely old man whom the children called Mr Chocolate. He would walk out from the village to our house bearing a few bars of chocolate for the girls. In the hot weather these had melted into the wrappers by the time he reached our house but they were nonetheless most welcome. Mr Chocolate was a good student who already spoke French and Italian. He always did his homework perfectly but try as I would I could not persuade the man to *speak* English. He understood everything but was perhaps afraid of losing face by making a mistake if he actually spoke the language. I also taught a few women in their thirties, also non-islanders, and was surprised to find that they treated me as a sort of therapist to whom they could tell their woes. They did this in rapid Greek so that I did not understand half of what they said. I tried to get them to get things off their chests, as it were, in English. After all, this was supposed to be an English lesson. That would work for a while and then they'd lapse into Greek once more. They felt confined, restricted by the island mores, which in those days meant that unmarried women had to be chaperoned and their every move was watched in case any scandal would ensue. *Why are you telling me all this?* I would ask. *Because you are a young, modern European woman*, they said.

Other students were two young male teachers from the gymnasium. Neither was from Paros and I was astonished to learn in conversation with them that both of their aged mothers travelled to Paros from Lesbos once or twice a month to bring their babies a supply of fresh clothes and home-cooked meals. *Can you not use a washing machine? Can't you go to the laundry here? Can you not cook?* I asked. *You are twenty-five years old, for God's sake.* They told me that they felt sorry for Irish men if all Irish women were like me!

Mixing with my students and with the parents of the children in Orla's class gave me an entrée, and insights into Parian society which I would not otherwise have had. This also forced me to learn enough Greek to communicate with them and to help Orla with her homework. She had quite a lot of homework to do for a six-year-old child and she learned so much that at Christmas when there were exams at school she did very well. Mothers would stop me in the street asking, *Posos vathmos echi?* I hadn't a clue what that meant, so I asked Orla and she told me that they had had tests and that the teacher had written numbers on her copy book. *What numbers?* I asked. *9 and 10*, she said. I told the inquiring mothers, *She got 9 and 10.* Oh, they exclaimed, *Top marks! A little xeni. Brava.*

Near the end of our second year on the island we decided, for various reasons, that we would go back to Ireland. Our mothers had come to visit and we realised how much the children missed their grandparents and vice versa. We also decided that we would always return to Paros. For that to happen we knew we had to buy a house here. We would not want to spend summers in rooms rooms. The house- hunt and purchase is another whole long story. We finally managed to buy a ruin in Isterni, in those days as remote as Timbuktu. And this is where we have spent the last thirty-four happy summers. Orla was married on the island in 2006. She still remembers a lot of her Greek, though she can no longer write it. She had to unlearn the Greek alphabet when she went back to school in Dublin so that she could write in English.

The Paros of the late 1970s was an island where old traditions still operated, where the bulk of the people were farmers and fishermen, where there were few roads and fewer cars, where donkeys and mules were everywhere, where one could only buy local food in season, where there was no electricity or running water in many parts of the island, where the tourist wave had yet to engulf the place, where unmarried women were chaperoned, where *prikas* (dowries) were very much the custom, where there were relatively few resident foreigners, most of whom knew, or knew of, each other, where there was great spirit of helpfulness among us.

Most of the resident foreigners were young. I hardly knew anyone over thirty-five, with the exception of the wonderful American women I mentioned earlier. I have already told stories about some of these residents and friends in my book and will not repeat them here. Not many islanders spoke English in those days, as French was the foreign language taught in the schools, so it was more necessary for us foreigners to learn Greek if we wanted to be part of the society in which we lived. There were no fast or frequent ferries to the island; the journey from Piraeus on the rust buckets that sailed took up to seven hours. There was, of course, no airport; there were no luxury villas, no swimming pools, no fancy shops and restaurants and no health clinic either. Life has become easier in so many ways for Parians, both native and foreign: there are so many more activities for old and young, better health, educational, sporting and transport facilities. Greece was not in the EU and the drachma was the currency. Rampant borrowing and building were virtually unknown, as was major debt. For many Parians, as well as for us xenia, life was simpler and perhaps a good deal less stressful in those days. Yes indeed, there are aspects of our lives on the island in the two years in which we lived there full-time from 1977 to 1979 which I still think about a bit wistfully. What is wrong, after all, with a little touch of nostalgia now and then?

Fionnuala Brennan,
Dublin,
Ireland,
February 2012

Taverna Damianos and Hotel Ventouris, 1975
Courtesy of Annelize Goedbloed

CYCLADIC SHORELINE

By Rory Brennan

A shimmering mosaic of stones,
Shells, old pottery and bones
　Patterns the seabed.
The centuries they took to reach
This abandoned rim of beach
　Revolve within my head.

Fossil, seawreck, artifact – here
Lies the haft of wild Achilles' spear.
　The fingers of his hand
Still curl like iron brackets round
This spine of wood. Stand on this ground,
　inhale the land.

Listen as the wind tells where
The ghosts of gods incise the air
　And speak of the unspoken.
Through the caves of allegory
Poseidon chariots the sea
　To yield another token.

The water fondles the long strands
Of seaweed with instinctive hands
  And disentangles there
A rejected lover's marble face
Implacably alone in the dark lace
Of Ariadne's hair.

A fleck of black flits on the sky.
Craft taught old Daedalus to fly
  And discount luck,
To judge, unlike his son. The white scar
Sudden in the blue, a plunging star,
  And Icarus unstuck.

Clay, rock, water, light — the landscape
Moulded man to mould his own shape
  These fictive deities;
Extraordinary and weak, enduring and absurd,
Their power recalls in a euphonic word
  Our repetitious ways.

Thus beauty makes the rational concede
To the imagination's darker need
  And bow to her.
The fiery images complete their dance,
The sun, saluting, dips his lance
  On copperplated water.

CHARLOTTE'S STORY · 1984
By Charlotte Carlin

Charlotte 1984

Ah, the scent of Paros, that very special airborne mixture of aromas from all the herbs combined, that scent, ah, is the first agent to welcome you back. And then, next, comes the wind. Like a lover's soft hands it caresses your face and your hair and it tears at your clothes. You are prepared for the meeting, though. Looking out through the small window, as the pilot steers the plane to a landing position, you have already seen him, the wind, running like velvet through the green fields of tall grasses and you cannot wait to expose your whole body to his embrace. Pleasures of anticipation, however, as it is still spring and his arms are chilly.

Oh, to be back. A hitherto absent sensation of warmth and gratitude conquers my weary body, worn out after a long trip from a faraway country; a smile spreads from head to toe, expanding my whole being. Thank God this taxi driver is not talkative. Or if he is, thank god the taxi is full of other people he can talk to. I've only been gone for five months but this homecoming is sacred and needs to be savoured in silence.

At this time of the year the island itself is enveloped in silence, bracing itself for the hordes of tourists that will soon transform its slumbering existence into a roaring inferno of cars and motorcycles.

But meanwhile, meanwhile, this hilly landscape is incredibly green, roadsides and fields are adorned with red poppies, white and yellow daisies, blue thistles and sea lavenders, pink morning glories, bushy curry plants, elegant Queen Anne's lace, fennel and chamomile. There's a woman collecting herbs from the roadside, a shepherd in a field, guiding his flock, a man on donkey, two doves courting on a wire.

All of the above is still here despite the transformations this tiny pearl of an island has gone through in the course of the twenty-eight years that have transpired since my husband, Carl, and I first set foot here. The small eighteen-seater aircraft has grown into a thirty-six seater; houses, developments and shops have mushroomed – many of which are now standing empty. But the scent, the wind, the green fields, the shepherd, the woman, the donkey, the doves – they are all still here, as is my profound love for this place on earth.

But why, they ask – those who have never been here - why, of all the thousands of Greek islands scattered around the Mediterranean, why did you chose Paros? Well, sometimes it feels as if, in spite of all our plans to the contrary, Paros chose us.

In 1984 Carl and I decided to leave Greenland, where we had both been working for five years. We wanted a break and we wanted to do something 'wild' before starting a new job somewhere else. So we bought a four-meter long German rubber dinghy and had it sent, by truck, from Copenhagen to Athens. Our plan was to find a quiet corner in the huge port of Piraeus, open up two small containers full of a jigsaw puzzle that was later to be a two-seat dinghy with a forty horsepower outboard motor. In that little thing it was our plan to go from Piraeus, around the Peloponnese, all the way up to Corfu and back through the Corinth Canal to Piraeus. We had two months and a lot of guts to do something like two thousand nautical miles on a very capricious Mediterranean Sea at the height of the Meltemi season. And we had two canisters full of fuel in the back of boat, two sleeping bags and a tent for all the deserted beaches that were to be our residence throughout the trip.

The fishermen in the little port where we spent three days assembling the dinghy before the trip all shook their heads and said the whole idea was pure folly and that a trip like that couldn't be done in a boat that size and shape. We knew better, of course; we had *read* that it could be done. The fanzine dedicated to that special type of dinghy was full of descriptions of hazardous adventures and what's more, we had tried out the boat in the icy waters of Greenland.

Although we were to discover that there is a huge difference between a quiet icy fjord and a wild Mediterranean, we knew that the boat had been strong enough to carry the three reindeer we were allowed to shoot on our yearly hunting trips.

We arrived in Athens by plane two weeks ahead of the boat and had planned to stay in the city the entire time. It was only our second visit to Greece; the first had been to Crete and we had never really been to Athens. The mere name of that city conjured up thousands of images, which, for someone from the cold North, were almost equivalent to the stories of *Arabian Nights*. Athens for me, even the old airport, was an instant attraction; I loved the atmosphere, the smells, the people, the chaos; it all reminded me of South America, but it had one big advantage over that continent: it was Europe, which meant that somewhere in a faraway corner of my psyche it was me. Like France was me. And Spain. Actually, planning that whole trip around Greece had been a second choice. Our first choice had been Spain. We both spoke the language and we wanted to sail the boat on the Guadalquivir River, a nice and different way to see the country that we knew so well. So, one day in Barcelona, we had walked into a bookshop and asked for a book about navigating the Guadalquivir. "That river is not negotiable", was the answer. "Really? Well, what river is, then? Didn't Columbus...?" We were happy to settle for any of them. "None of them," came the disappointing answer, "none of them".

Which was why we were now in Athens.

It was hot. We did what we had to do, contacted the shipping agency responsible for getting the boat through customs, found a quiet corner of Piraeus for later use, and decided that once we returned from the trip, in October, we would 'do' Athens. So, once all the arrangements had been made to receive the boat, we took off to Paros. Paros? Why Paros? It couldn't have been more haphazard. On the stopover in Sophia we had met this wonderfully weird optometrist from Denmark. He had suggested we spent the waiting time on the island of Paros instead of Athens. "Far too hot in Athens," he had said "and Paros is in the Cyclades, off your planned route."

On the overcrowded ferry to Paros, a journey which in those days took somewhere between six to seven hours, I read in Fodor's that the place to go was a village named Naoussa. Lawrence Durrell seemed to agree. Although his description was very brief, he did call it *"a delightful little fishing village with the usual Venetian fort cresting it"*. I adored Durrell. During the dark winter months in Greenland, whilst preparing for the trip, his books had been my Aladdin's lamp: every evening the genie came out to make everything rich and shining; the whole of Greece became shrouded in the purple golden light of imagined sunsets. The way Durrell described 'To Phos', the light, blew my mind and I can still remember the way he described its effect on the material world: as if everything was *prime*, seen for the first time, as if a god had just exclaimed *'Let there be donkey'*. It was intelligent, perceptive and hilarious at the same time, and it stuck in my mind. I couldn't wait to see things that way!

For sure, the main town, Paroikia, was to be avoided. Durrell, in describing Paroikia, excels in flowerpots of linguistic elegance. I loved: *'the feeling of zestful ease.... dazzling white streets... criss-crossed and stitched with interconnecting lanes of pure whiteness,* like *simply felicitous afterthoughts'*. I also adored the next one where he describes the whole town as being *'scribbled over by an absent-minded god'*, but my absolute best was: *'Every day, when you awake, it seems quite fresh, as though finished in the night and opened to the public just this morning.'* So why was Paroikia to be avoided - with all this glory and splendour? Because Paroikia was where the feast of the Assumption was celebrated on the 15th of August *'with as much fervour as it is on Tinos'*. And Tinos, we had read, was the Lourdes of modern Greece.

Well, he could have fooled me. When, after fighting for a taxi, we ended up sharing with as many people as could fit in, we arrived in Naoussa on that very holy day, it looked as if that *little delightful fishing village* was the Lourdes of all of Europe's countries combined. Naoussa was a Babel of tongues, bursting at the seams; people stood, sat, walked like sardines in a tin. The entire European tourism seemed to have congregated in Naoussa, and we were very, very lucky to find an obscure room somewhere in the village for two nights after which, come hell or high water, it was out. After trying to find a table for dinner that night in a village whose narrow streets were like a four-lane human highway, we both agreed that that was ok. Come hell or high water, out it was.

The problem the following day was that you couldn't rent any form of vehicle. Not a car, not a motorbike, not a scooter, not a bicycle, not a donkey, nothing. So we started walking out of the village and got onto to a tarred road leading south. After a few kilometres a turn-off to the left looked as if it would lead us to the sea. More or less twenty minutes further on, following a hot, very hot, dirt road we finally arrived at a tiny little place called Ambelas - a few scattered houses, two or three tavernas and a small hotel. No people, no noises; just the sea and the wind; just the pure whiteness of a simply felicitous afterthought. The place felt like out of a Garcia Marquez' novel; in this place, for sure, no one would ever write to the colonel.

We had lunch at the taverna by the sea. A few tables, fresh seafood, the sound of exquisite music mingled with the whistle of the bamboo leafed roof. Unclouded sky, dark blue sea, the sun beating down on faraway Naxos. Maybe we could get a room in the small hotel?

A lovely, elderly lady in what turned out to be the Ventouris family's hotel understood from our few Greek words that we wanted a hotel room. No problem. Only two rooms were occupied, so we had fourteen to choose from. No need. They were all small and sparsely furnished, and they were available.

We stayed in this paradise a little over a week, got to know the other two occupants of the hotel, an Irish couple, brother and sister. Some Greek friends of theirs joined the party, and every lunch was taken in the taverna by the sea. After a late siesta we would all meet up again under the huge fig tree in the yard of the hotel's taverna.

Back in Piraeus we assembled the boat and took off on an incredible adventure. A whole (unpublished) book was later written about the trip; here I just want to mention that we spent two months on deserted beaches and only booked into hotels when the towels and clothes got too thick from the salt water.

And that at times our little rubber dinghy climbed walls of waves which from our perspective at the bottom seemed to be at least five meters high. After completing the trip and safely back in Athens, we both said: never more Greece. Why we said that I actually do not remember now, almost thirty years later. Maybe because Greece, at the time, was not really geared to that massive influx of people? A fact that on the one hand constituted its great charm but on the other left the Greeks exhausted and irritable at the end of the season. Wouldn't that explain why, in late September and beginning of

October they almost threw the food at you? Or maybe we felt that after such a long voyage we had seen it all? Maybe because Spain was really where we should be? We had previously been looking at houses in Tenerife and probably hadn't discarded that dream yet. Yes, Spain was where we should be.

The following year, still working on the book, I persuaded Carl to go back to Paros. I felt that I needed to get in touch with the whole atmosphere again in order to get on with my writing; I needed to smell, feel and touch Greece again. Once again we stayed in Ambelas, spent the days on the beach or driving around the island. We met up with our Irish and Greek friends for lunch at Damianos and for dinner at Ventouris.

Two years on we started looking for land to build. We had made the 'mistake' of staying more than two weeks on the island after which, as the saying goes, you are hooked. The lovely, elderly lady whom we now knew as old Eleni. as opposed to her granddaughter young Eleni, showed us a few places for sale, and I remember there was one in particular she was eager for us to buy: it was right under the multitude of electric poles that supply Naxos with electricity from Paros. She was a very practical woman who had lived most of her life without electricity, so she must have thought that by living right under the singing wires we would be spared a lot of the inconveniences she had experienced in her life.

Finally, with the help of one of our Greek friends, we found a piece of land in pristine and uninhabited Filizi, close to the white cliffs, the Aspros Gremnos. From Greenland we travelled back to the island in the dead of winter to a dark and deserted Paros, signed all the papers on the 23rd December at the notary's office in Paroikia, and spent that Christmas in a damp hotel room going through tons of house and décor magazines.

On the few sunny days of that holiday we drove out to Filizi, accompanied by our newly found architect. Together we designed what was to become our dream house, situated on the seaboard, surrounded by miles after miles of sometimes green, sometimes yellow fields, depending on the season. How long would it take before we could move in? Well, let's see – six months for the adia, the building licence, to be approved on Naxos and something like six months to build. A year, give or take? If not next year around Christmas, then surely the summer after that.

Well, the summer after that came and went. As did the next. And the next. And the next. For five years after that exiting Christmas when we bought the land, we kept coming back to stay at the Ventouris family hotel in Ambelas. Kyria Eleni was patience herself teaching us Greek while, out of season, all the elderly ladies came to her place to embroider bridal linen for a forthcoming wedding. She was hospitality incarnate when, one late September morning, we arrived out of the blue, exhausted from a long haul flight, to find the little hotel fully booked. Not knowing what to do because a nearby hotel was also full, we just sat there in the taverna, leaning across the table, trying to get some sleep amongst all the breakfasting guests, waiting for a solution to materialize as it always does in Greece. After a little while, we were tapped on the shoulder and shown to a big mattress Eleni had quietly placed under the huge fig tree that was the pride of the taverna. So there we slept for hours, breakfasting guests turning into lunching guests, and woke up later, figs scattered on and around the mattress, to a perfect solution that I no longer remember.

We kept coming back to the little Ventouris Hotel from all over the world. We travelled to Paros from Greenland, where we had gone back to work for another couple of years, from Copenhagen, from Seattle, from Buenos Aires, from Cape Town. Paros became the centre of the world, a fixed point in our ever-changing landscape and Kyria Eleni was always there – with one grandchild, then with two, and eventually with three.

We came back for one week, for two weeks, for three months at a time to inspect the extremely slow construction. A couple of years into the project I took a friend, the only other foreigner we knew of on that side of the island, out to have a look at our still unfinished house. Actually at that stage it was only a basement, but what a basement! Fifteen meters by ten and four meters high it looked more like a cathedral to us. We had no idea why we were to have a basement that size – it couldn't even be turned into spare bedrooms because there was no room above ground to put in windows, so why on earth had the architect commissioned a monster like that? We had meeting after meeting with him, before we smelled a rat – a huge rat the size of another cathedral: quite coincidentally we happened to get hold of a piece of handwritten paper that turned out to be the contract between the architect and the guy who delivered concrete. The 0 in the number 10 had been turned into a 9, which meant that instead of paying 10 thousand drachmas per cubic meter of concrete, which was the price at the time - we paid 19 thousand of which the architect got 9 thousand – on top of his usual salary. No wonder he wanted to use a hell of a lot of concrete, and since we had commissioned the house to be built of stone, where could he put it other than in the basement? My friend was obviously always looking at the bright side of things, because her only comment was that you can never have enough room for storage! A few months later, though, she sent us a letter in Greenland to say that we had better come to Paros ASAP.

It turned out that the construction of our dream house had been thrust into the hands of a gambler! It is normal, in Greece, for the architect to get a commission from the subcontractors, but this guy took the cake. The fellow, who had been recommended to us by a friend from Athens, turned out to be a gambler and a crook, who defrauded us of an unknown amount of money. Our big mistake had been to choose a 'foreigner', that is someone *not* from the island. We had not checked his reputation here, only relied on the fact that he was recommended to us by someone we knew – who was also not from the island! The locals were outraged and came to our rescue: just before the whole story turned into a Kafkan court case, help arrived in the form of even more fraud with another project after which our gambler was forced to leave the island. And the so-called friend who had recommended him, and who had been coming to Paros every summer for fifteen years, suddenly changed location too.

Eventually, after five, six years of hope and despair – the concrete story was only one of many horror stories, but this is a *short* story and not a novel – we could finally move into the house in Filizi.

The year was now 1992 and still there were no houses between our house and the little taverna 'To Kima' a few kilometres to the South, and there were no houses between our house and the village of Santa Maria a few kilometres to the North. There also was no water. Even more concrete had been poured into enormous underground cisterns, but, alas, the inclination of the roof tilted the wrong way, so that instead of feeding the cisterns, all the rainwater fed the garden. Never mind. For a small fortune we could have the water wagon fill the cisterns and for free we could have repeated lessons in water saving - having by now learned to look at the bright side. Also we had no electricity, but that too had an up-side: the endless painting of doors, windows and shutters had to stop well before sundown, when we would turn on the generator for a decent shower, light the candles, pour an ouzo and watch the sunset reflect in window after window on Naxos right across from us. Shortly after that, the stars came out. We would push back the reclining chairs and gaze in naked wonder at a night sky covered with millions and millions of twinkling stars. When someone at some stage asked us whether we had a TV set, we said no but we had Naxos and an immaculate night sky untouched by the lights of civilization. He thought that was a very funny answer. We didn't.

Did we think that this pristine Paros life would last forever? I think we did. When we bought the land, four plots had been for sale, but our Greek neighbours to the back of the house who eventually had their houses built, seemed to share our values – or if they didn't, we didn't notice. The big silence necessary to enjoy the sounds of the wind, of birds singing, of seagulls crying, of donkeys braying was still present throughout the days, and the nights were still full of stars.

The advent of first electricity and much later water from the municipality was perceived and experienced as something of a revolution. We got electricity in the late nineties and water in the naughties and we didn't think twice about it. It was an improvement through and through. Not only did we appreciate it so much more for having managed without these mod cons for so long, we also felt privileged to have experienced this huge transition from a semi medieval lifestyle, as we jokingly called it, to a modern one.

Until one night, when I drove home from the village and from a distance saw a cluster of bright lights in the horizon. Completely disorientated – we were used to a vast darkness most of the way from Ambelas to our house – I thought that these were the lights of a never before noticed village somewhere in the distance. But no, they were just the beginning of lots of other lights to come, lights that would eventually outshine a couple of million stars. Little did we think when we, delighted by a kind of compressed evolution, plugged in the first lamp and were able to read at night, that Filizi with the advent of electricity and water would become posh and pricey; that the salty blue sea, the island's protagonist, would be reduced to a backdrop for freshwater swimming pools on an island with constant water problems; that shrubs and natural vegetation, which for

thousands of years had adapted to a low rain area, would be replaced by water consuming lawns; that dirt roads would be asphalted and streetlights put up.
Naïve? Of course! Wonderful to imagine that paradise can be found and last, not lost.

One day we visited a couple in Ysterni, once a small village whose original inhabitants had to move out because their wells filled with salt water. Eventually new people moved in. This time not farmers but foreigners, mostly. Greeks from Athens, who, seen with island eyes, are also foreigners, and other Europeans. People who, for the most part, wanted to preserve and maintain the old farmhouses, who restored them with great love and care – and an incredible amount of physical labour. Access to some of these old farmhouses was by ancient donkey paths, and although we had been given detailed directions by the couple, we did not manage, first time around, to find the farmhouse they had rented for the month of September. When we finally did climb the donkey path and crossed the yellow rocks full of caper plants growing straight out of the rock walls, we were faced with the breathtaking view of two volcano-shaped mountains rising out of the plains below, the sea forming two turquoise-blue bays at their feet.

We were given a tour of this incredibly beautiful farmhouse, whose owners for many years had spent all their holidays – and probably all their money – to achieve the complete opposite of what was going on in Filizi. We were told that the picturesque old marble sink in the kitchen, along with all the other building material that went into restoring the house, had been transported up the donkey path on donkey back, and we imagined summer after summer of blood, sweat and tears – interspersed with frequent visits to the beach below, picnic baskets in hand.

"And this ruin next door?" I heard my husband ask, pointing to a badly maintained old farmhouse surrounded by a mishmash of dilapidated yellow-grey rock stones that had once served as stables and outhouses. "Oh that? Well, that's for sale, has been for many years now. No one seems to dare tackle a project like that. Why don't you buy it? You look like a man who loves projects."

I cringed inwardly. How did he know? Carl does love projects, but my God, I wasn't going to go through the nightmare of building on Paros a second time. I started figuring out how many years I might have left to live, and asked myself if another big part of them were going to be spent painting shutters – figuratively speaking. 'Painting shutters' had come to be a euphemism for all the things that prevented you from being the idle tourist spending your holiday relaxing on beaches, tavernas and hotel rooms. The connotation was two-fold: it meant either spending your whole holiday painting and maintaining. Or it meant running around to authorities that always asked you to come back the next day – with yet another piece of documentation they had forgotten to mention the first time you visited. Conversations at the few dinner parties we managed to squeeze in were not about democracy in ancient Greece, but about the price of labour and where to buy doorknobs, tiles and toilet seats. Over the past few years, we had slowly moved away from that kind of holidaymaking and started enjoying our always too short time on the island. To start all over again? You would have to be the fool on this hill.

The broken window in the back of the decrepit farmhouse was too small for Carl to pass through, so I climbed in and opened the window in the room facing the sea and the two volcano-shaped mountains. The view was tremendous and made me think of two pointed hills on a US military base in Greenland called MMM by the soldiers. The letters stood for Marilyn Monroe Memorial. I quickly relegated the thought as sacrilegious and forgave myself for making fun as a way of preventing myself from falling in love with the place.

The property itself was a mass of unspoiled land with old dry-walled terraces laid in a hilly landscape of indigenous shrubs and bushes. The shrubs would scratch your bare legs as you walked through them and compensate you with the scent of thyme, oregano, sage, juniper and rockroses. As if to convince us that you *can* fall in love a second time, two falcons soared in the blue sky high above us.

Whenever the lights, lawns and pools reached this area – and they would, we knew that the size and position of this piece of land would ensure that whoever bought it would not suffer from such intrusions as they would all remain at a safe distance. Somewhere in this hilly landscape you would always be able to watch the stars.

We bought it. We gave in and permitted ourselves to fall in love a second time.

Like with all kinds of love one tends to ask oneself what it is all about. What is it that makes this love so special? What is it that will gladly make you go through so much trouble – even a second time? When a fellow Parosphile told me that she would sometimes, during the winter in her faraway country, call her vacant home on Paros just to feel some kind of contact with her beloved island, I was not surprised. I could easily have performed the same folly.

For me the very special thing about Paros is a deep resonance between my inner and outer, soul and environment. It is a resonance I don't experience anywhere else in the world. My breathing becomes like a child's; deep into the lungs like a child's first breath after an inconsolable throb, the one that indicates that all is well – once again.

There is a sense of being totally at ease in my skin, afraid of nothing – or almost nothing! – together with a strong sense of feminine strength and power. There is, in spite of everything we went through, a feeling that what you are exposed to here, are never problems - they are challenges to be solved.

There is, furthermore, a deep feeling of gratitude for having found this place and for being allowed to stay here. Gratitude towards the infinite beauty of the island on a windless day when the sea twinkles like a diamond through a magnifying glass. Or on any other day - beauty being the all-pervading quality of Paros and humanity being the all-pervading quality of the Parians. No doubt Aeschylus, Euripides and Sophocles all visited this island.

But let us not forget Lawrence Durrell: *Every day, when you awake, it seems quite fresh, as though finished in the night and opened to the public just this morning.* Maybe he hit it right on the nail. Maybe he was not talking of Paroikia only, but of the whole of Paros. Maybe that feeling of freshness is what makes us breathe.

Charlotte Carlin
Eilandia, South Africa
June, 2011

View from Filizi towards Ambelas, 1986
Courtesy of C. Carlin

JEAN'S STORY · 1985
By Jean Polyzoides

John and Jean, 1985

The Paros Experience

It's two-thirty in the morning, late even for Greece – and I am looking at a mass of stars and a huge full moon. It is the August full moon which the Greeks insist is the lucky one of the year and the largest. It is almost hypnotizing and it makes me very reluctant to leave it for the company of my now very sleepy husband. The evening has been a full one, although after over ten years of living here on the island of Paros we have got used to the Greek way of fitting in several "events" in a twenty-four hour period, and has set me thinking about the real differences in the life-style and attitude that I now experience everyday living as an "ex-pat" on a Greek island.

This evening we spent part of it listening to a concert in the village square in the fishing port of the island, Naoussa, where we sat on cardboard boxes with a plank across for stability, and more in front of us for drinks and snacks. The square was absolutely packed, it is normally used for basket-ball, and a children's playground, with a walking area from one side of the village to the other trendy clubs along the "river bed". The singer was the reason we had come as it was her first important solo concert. We had first known her as a teenager and it was fifteen years since she had sung at our wedding. Now she had "made it big", being accompanied by the one of the best-known violinists for this type of music. There were hundreds of people to hear her sing, applaud her performance and dance for several hours.

It was then that I realized just how different it was here compared to going out to any sort of event in England, or probably most of northern Europe. It was not the primitiveness (but quite comfortable) seating arrangements, the lateness of the performance or the casual attitude. That can still happen at an outdoor music festival in England, but what can't happen anymore, is the joining together of people of several generations, from three years old to an elderly gentlemen with a stick in one hand and holding the hand of a young tourist from Norway or Sweden in the other. There were no worries about your child's safety, playing with the crowd, dancing faster and faster as the music increased, no worries that your car was going to be damaged in a car park by someone who thinks it is clever to put a scratch with a penknife down the side, and certainly no worries that there would be any violence or excessive drinking.

It made me feel emotional seeing children of all ages and several nationalities, as well as locals and Athenians, young and old, dancing and celebrating together without a care.

The last part of the evening was spent at the house of an orthopedic surgeon, the person who had first introduced my husband to Paros after he had visited England with a sabbatical from his hospital in Athens. We had arrived for "dinner" at 12.30 after slipping away from the dancing and singing. The house was several miles away on the opposite coast of the island, with magnificent views of the bay. Andreas had been born on the island, his father had been headmaster of the school. This was in the 1940s and 50s when the Greeks were still in political turmoil and very poor as a nation, particularly on the islands. Tourism was almost unknown then in the Cyclades, you had to be pretty determined to get to Paros with only one boat a day from the mainland which took ten or twelve hours, and only a few "rooms" or apartments to rent when you got there.

Andreas and his friends all did well at school, and he went off to study medicine in

Athens, but never lost his love for Paros and came whenever he could to spend a few days wandering along a deserted beach, or walking the hills amongst the smells of oregano, thyme, and mostly of course the sea. He built a house on Paros, in a beautiful setting with gardens full of plants and flowers and verandas all round, and when we arrived at 12.30 no-one even seemed to notice the fact that we started to eat our steak and salad when they were eating dessert. Later we reminisced about my first visit to Paros and I realised that we would never have been living in our house by the sea, spending miraculous evenings gazing at the ferry boats arriving and watching the stars, which seemed to increase and become clearer every night, if it had not been for him.

The first Paros Adventure.

This may sound like the beginning of one of those splendid Enid Blyton stories but it really was an adventure, and what an introduction it proved to be to the total disorganization and virtual anarchy of the Greeks. As people, they are amazing, so generous with their time, their friendship, they always share their food and good times with the xenos, the foreigner, but when it comes to advance planning they are last in the line. They attribute this to their need to be independent and to show that they will not be dictated to.

It is only when you think that they had so many different occupiers, only being liberated in mainland Greece on 13th October 1944 by the British Army who entered Athens with George Jellicoe riding on a bicycle to the main square in Athens to celebrate freedom from the Nazis, that you begin to understand why they are like this and just do not want to plan ahead. But when you are completely unaware of this, and trying as I was, to organize for twelve people to get to an island for Greek Easter, with no knowledge of where Paros even was, apart from a map and the stories I had heard from my partner

John, it was somewhat of a challenge. The reason we were going in a group was so that a friend who was a general practioner and who did marathon swims for charity, decided one dark and wet January evening in England, after sharing a good dinner and several glasses of good wine, that he would do a short swim from Paros to the neighbouring island of Antiparos, to raise money for the local Health Centre in Paros.

We decided to have a night in Athens on the way and catch the ferry boat the following afternoon. Now, in the days of on-line booking, this could be done by a six-year old, but then there were no advance bookings for the ferries unless you went to a travel agent in Piraeus to do it, with cash. We had no idea that would prove a problem, and anyway we had three days before Easter so we had time to wait for another ferry if the first one was full. I booked a hotel for all of us, including Christopher, the swimmer and his wife with their two teenagers, a Scottish businessman and his wife, and an Italian couple who had accompanied Chris on several swims. We had a wonderful evening and introduced them to Andreas who was accompanying the swim on his yacht.

The organization then began to seem like a marathon itself, with the first hurdle being that we did not realize that all the ferry boats had been booked for months as people who came from Paros and worked in Athens wanted to return to their family to celebrate. However, with a lot of persuading, gentle and then not-so-gentle, with a final desperate plea for help from a tourist agency, we made it and got the tickets. It was going to take eight hours but we had booked cabins, could play cards, chat and rest when we wanted to.

Athens seemed to be in a state of turmoil, I had never seen so many people "shouting" at each other at the same time, gesticulating, competing with the noise, old cars in need of a replacement exhaust, and loud Greek music coming from every one of them, especially the taxis. But I loved the excitement, the constant movement, even the aggression and impatience of the shopkeepers and coffee bar owners. It was all so different from my quiet suburban life. The first evening was magical, sitting looking at the Acropolis under a very starry sky with the moon almost directly over the Parthenon encouraging you to imagine the processions and celebrations that had taken place there when it was in its glory of the Periclean period.

Suddenly John started an animated discussion with the waiter at the huge ice-cream parlour at the foot of the Acropolis, and told us that there was a union strike of the ferryboat workers and all boats were cancelled "indefinitely". We were all so happy and excited that we tried to dismiss this catastrophic possibility, or maybe my memory is playing tricks and John just tried to make us feel that as he said – and still says – anything is possible in Greece! How often has that proved right ...

Next morning we went to the main ferry booking office, leaving the others to wander around Monasteraki, the market area of Athens which has a wonderful gaiety about it, it is always packed with people, not necessarily buying but just soaking in the busy atmosphere with various smells coming from the shops selling herbs, the various kebab shops and bakeries, and gazing at the dozens of jewelry shops. At the booking office we were told that the strike was indefinite and if we had to guarantee getting to Paros for the Good Friday celebration the only possibility was to get a flight. At that time the flights to Paros were by a sixteen-seater plane, two a day, so we assumed that all the flights would be booked, but we were told that we could charter our own plane for the same price as buying sixteen tickets. That sounded a real jet-setting idea, as well as a very practical solution, so we went off to Olympic who said yes, we could do exactly that, and it would leave at 4pm. Eureka, we had the answer, but, and it was a very big but, as in those days in Greece they did not accept credit cards, there were no cash machines, and we needed to get the money on Good Friday when all the banks were closed. Inspiration came in the form of a sign saying American Express Office at the top of a building in Constitution Square. We went up and gave our American Express card, they gave us the money (so many drachma notes I literally filled my handbag with them), we went and paid Olympic and told everyone to pack their bags.

Of course, there had to be another problem, or it would not be Greece! We had to check-in at a special desk, so feeling very important, we took all our cases and the buoyancy floaters and other things for the boat, and reported to the desk. The allotted time came, we went out onto the tarmac to our small plane, but what were those two suitcases doing at the bottom of the steps? They belonged to Esther, the swimmer's daughter and myself, and made the aircraft overweight, despite the fact that we had a couple of extra seats which were empty. However, they promised that the cases would be delivered on the next available plane (visions of borrowing underwear flashed through my mind at this stage) and we boarded the aircraft.

We flew below the clouds. the first time I had ever experienced this, and it was spectacular, with a wine coloured sea, small islands dotted with bright white houses, small boats and larger tankers and freighters, with dozens of yachts coming from the harbour of Piraeus. Of course, I did not really believe that the cases would arrive, and was fully prepared to have to do a quick shop when we got to Paros, and in fact was quite looking forward to that – although the next day when we went exploring I realized that the three dress shops at the time on Paros were not exactly what I would have hoped for! After forty minutes the pilot informed us that we would be landing at Paros airport, and as we gazed down and came in steeply to land on the very short runway that almost reached the sea, I knew that the island was going to have an influence on my life, there was something special about it, and that the people would become my friends. We split up into two groups, the boys, John and I staying with his friend Babis in a newly-built, modern, large villa right on the sea. The others stayed at a small traditional hotel which we could walk to through some very old tamarisk, eucalyptus and acacia trees which were overhanging perilously across parts of the marble cliff. We raced to get ready for the Good Friday church service that we were so looking forward to, we went into the Ektapilyani Church of The Virgin Mary, at eleven-thirty, coming out just before midnight and following the procession down to the port, meeting with the two other churches from Paroikia, and then going around the town. The atmosphere in the church was solemn. The bells tolled mournfully, with everyone dressed in dark clothes.

The church had everything draped in purple cloth, the lights were dim, and the men were on the right side of the church and the women on the left. We went upstairs to the gallery to watch, and where we could all stand together. There was a flower-covered bier with candles, signifying Christ's journey from the Cross, which was taken around the church three times, with only candles to light the way, and then carried very slowly, accompanied by the school band, playing slow liturgical music and then Chopin's Funeral March, down to the port, where hundreds of people gathered. At exactly midnight there was a sudden hush as all three biers, one from each of the churches in the town, and their accompanying congregations met at the windmill in front of the port. They joined together and everyone followed the slow procession of the three candle-lit, beautifully hand-decorated biers carried on the shoulders of young men, around the small streets. The atmosphere was sombre but there was a subdued sense of anticipation of the days to follow. On returning to the villa we found our Easter present had arrived, the suitcases had, as promised, been delivered literally to the door by the manager of the airport on his way to the evening service. What kindness we had already been shown here on Paros.

Easter Saturday passed in a whirl of activity. We explored the town and the old Venetian castle built on the ruins of the Temple of Athena, watched the fishermen mending their nets, men playing backgammon in the kafenion and people finishing whitewashing their houses, a must for the Easter celebration. Our friend Babis is a meat merchant and for him it is the busiest day of the year, every family must have a lamb to put on the spit for the Easter Day itself. People were arriving at his shop with their long barbecue rods, he would thread them through the lamb and secure it with special screws and hinges, and they would leave carrying it over their shoulders. Some people had their lamb cooked at the oven of the fournos, the bakers, so some had to be prepared in pieces and taken there. The atmosphere was frenzied and exciting and we began to feel the same sense of anticipation as you do when you are a child on Christmas Eve. On our way to church we stopped to buy special candles, with little plastic holders, which we took with us so that we could, we were told, receive the Holy Light to bring us good health and fortune during the year.

The church service is again long and there is a sense of sadness in the church until at midnight the lights are turned-off completely and everyone leaves, including all the priests and bishop. The doors are closed and the senior priest or bishop knocks three times before going back in. After the Holy Light has been passed to everyone outside the church, the bells clang loudly, clashing together without any sense of rhythm, firecrackers thrown in the square outside, people shout loudly "Christos Anesti", meaning Christ has risen, and there is pandemonium as some people try to go back into the church and others try to leave to get to their home or taverna to eat the traditional soup and lamb. Yes, lamb at 2am... and as I know now from years of practice, after staggering to bed, the alarm rings only too quickly to get up and help light the fire for the barbecue and our own lamb.

The flame arrives by aeroplane from Jerusalem in the morning and is then distributed around Greece (you have to be a master of logistics to work that one out with all the small and large ferries involved). We have a little lantern with us to take the 'holy light' back home to light a special candleri with oil and wick after making a smoky cross three times on the marble above the front door.

However, twenty years ago I had no idea of all that hard work, it was just magical to see the light being brought in absolute silence from the church and then each candle held carefully as it was lit from one person to another to avoid being blown out by the wind. I have very vivid memories of that moment when I first saw the hundreds of lights in the quadrangle of the church, packed with people, young and old, babies in pushchairs and elderly people in wheelchairs, families, widows dressed in black mourning their lost ones, and the priests in their beautiful embroidered robes. The memory of that first year in Paros at Easter-time embedded itself so deeply in my memory that I try to recreate the same excitement and pleasure every year.

That Easter was a constant whirl with us all helping to cook the traditional lamb on the spit on Sunday and then the following day it was 'The Swim'. Everything started well. Chris dived into the water, anxious to be underway, and we gradually followed after maneuvering out of the busy harbour and going along the whole of the water-front of the main town of Paroikia. However, we suddenly realized we had no captain. Andreas had dived from the boat and made his way to shore, and the next thing we knew he was swimming back, using one arm, carrying a heavy tray of hot, freshly baked pastichio (baked pasta with mincemeat in tomato sauce), wrapped in several layers of foil and a gingham tea cloth, in his other hand, holding it well above the water. It was an incredible feat! And as for the smell, and the taste of this most Greek of all dishes, it was wonderful, in fact it was just too good, and we ate at least half of it on the way.

We made good time, but not as good as the swimmer, who had kept up a regular sixty a minute stroke rate and was well ahead of us – in fact so far ahead that he was idling time in the small bay when we got there, so that we could be on the beach to greet him. As he rose like a colossus from the water and made his way up the beach to greet us, a family who were having a late lunch on their veranda, shouted across to find out what was happening. Within minutes there were several families joining us and one of the women even stopped on the way in her garden to pick a bunch of early roses and presented them to Chris.

What a friendly and spontaneous gesture that was, something that has remained in our minds ever since, and certainly something he has never forgotten, in spite of the fact that he has become a legend in the world of marathon swimmers. That welcome in Antiparos he says has a special place in his heart.

The rest of that holiday passed by in a blur of meeting people, walks along golden, sandy, deserted beaches, seeing fields full of wild flowers and mountains of wonderful smelling bracken and herbs. We went to the marble mines, the oldest in the world, we made friends and talked about everything, and every day I fell more and more enchanted with Paros. However, after a week on returning to the UK the daily circle of hospital life which we both so enjoyed soon took over our lives again, but all the time I could not shake off the feeling that Paros was going to play an important part in my life. Something subtle had happened - it was if a seed had been planted and was taking root. Greece had somehow shown me a different way of thinking about life, I liked the attitude of the family towards each other, caring deeply about the daily life of their mothers, fathers and relatives and getting involved in their sicknesses and their celebrations; friends were just as important, and lasting friendships abounded.

I was right about the first moment I saw Paros and knew it would be somewhere special. Three years later we started building the house that is now our home and where we have shared many Easter celebrations with friends who come each year to renew the special bond they too have developed with Paros. The church where we spent that first night was where we chose to marry and the people we met over twenty years ago have become our close friends. John took over the Presidency of the Health Centre on a voluntary basis for a couple of years, he still sees patients whenever they ask, we helped to start the first public library on the island, and also are part of the Paros international arts circle – all things that have helped us be involved with the island we now call home.

Jean Polyzoides
Paros, Greece
April, 2012

Pouring newly trodden grape juice into a wineskin, 1973
Courtesy of Robin Brown

GAIL'S STORY · 1985
By Gail Saunders

Frank and Gail in 1985

People often claim allegiance to the place in which they were born: the town, the area ,or the country; however, there are a few beings that were born as free spirits. They are open, and define home by what they feel in a place. My late husband Frank and I were both blessed with this frame of mind and the accompanying heart stirrings. Although we each stepped onto Paros at different times, we both knew "this is home."

We first came to Greece in the '70s and fell in love with the country. Unfortunately, it was 1984, ten years later, before we returned. We had only two weeks for this particular trip, the standard time allotted for U.S. holidays. We chose to spend one week on Mykonos and the other on the Viking Star, a boat with about twenty passengers, traveling to different magical islands. Driving a jeep around Mykonos we came to the intersection of two remote dirt roads at the same time as a sporty open vehicle. Frank waved for the other driver to go ahead. Meanwhile, I was checking out this interesting looking character driving the other car. He was older and Greek, I speculated, with a jaunty turquoise hat perched on his head. He had one of the most fascinating faces I had ever seen. I had done a lot of portrait work in New Jersey and I knew I wanted to at least have the opportunity to sketch this man! I wasn't sure how much older he was, but definitely older than the pretty, young and vibrant woman beside him. My mind was racing - how can I at least get a photo of him? Then the man asked if we wanted some fresh bread. Yes! We followed them to a bakery. I whispered to Frank, "Don't let the poor Greek man pay for the bread." We learned his name was Costas and his girlfriend was Francine. He was Greek and she was Canadian. Costas insisted on buying the bread and suggested we continue to follow them to a picturesque bay and taverna on the unpopulated side of the island for some fresh fish. Why not?

We had an ouzo and black olives as Costas ordered fish to be prepared for us to eat after a swim and conversation on the golden beach. On the shore he regaled us with stories as his eyes sparkled. He was a real raconteur and bon vivant. His philosophies were fascinating as he painted pictures with his words and drew in the sand to punctuate his sagas. "There is a sea of humans, but very few stand out above the masses of bobbing heads," he proclaimed. Later I realized he was definitely one of the heads in my sea of humanity that rose above many others. He seemed to personify much of the Greek character. He surely was one of the most interesting humans I had met or have met since. After a delicious meal of fresh grilled fish we were invited to his home later for a drink at sunset.

Arriving at the address we were given I knew Costas was not a poor man. Wow! What a home with a fantastic sea view! Through further discussions we learned he had homes in eight countries. He was sixty-nine and Francine was twenty. It worked for them and, apparently, for his wife in Athens as well. We shared a magical week with them. He took us to a taverna where the owner picked up our table with all the dishes and glasses using only his teeth! The clientele were breaking plates to show their appreciation. After the table was set down, the owner tugged on my hand to dance with him alone in front of all the diners, so I went along. As we danced he went behind me and suddenly I was sitting on his shoulders. I kept dancing! I recall I had put hot pink geranium petals in my hair that evening. It was an exciting night.

The next day Costas took us out on a boat with a fisherman. The skiff was brightly painted in vivid reds and greens. We watched the captain gather fresh sea urchins, which we devoured with a squeeze of lemon on crusty bread, chased by ouzo. So many new experiences, impressions and ideas assaulted my being. I was dazed by the incredible light of Greece and the colours, which I wanted to eat and feel. This was living directly!

When Costas heard our plans for the boat for our second week he announced, "Rather come with me to the isle of Patmos and I will give you a house, a jeep, and a maid for the week." That night in bed Frank and I discussed our options: we couldn't get our money back from the boat trip, but we could do that another time. We might not be able to set *this* up again. We had to take this opportunity! We did go on the boat for two nights and then ferried to Patmos.

Costas owned five homes on Patmos. Ours overlooked the lacy land edges of the island where John wrote the Book of Revelations in his cave. As we sat on the terrace sipping a glass of champagne we realized we were living a fantasy. While there, we rode donkeys to Lambis beach, grabbing juicy figs from trees along the way. We attended dinner parties where taxi drivers and ambassadors were woven together creating sparkling evenings and conversations. In one of those conversations Marc, a gentleman who sat next to me one evening, said he was sleeping near a family chapel, had opened a wooden box, and was shocked to see it contained human bones. He went on to explain that he later learned that since land was so scarce people were exhumed after three years to make room in the family plot. The bones were cleaned by the eldest daughter in the family and placed in the box to be kept in or near the family chapel. Being the eldest daughter in my family, at that moment I was glad we weren't Greek! Nightly I filled my travel journal with colourful tidbits and rich experiences. Travel had always expanded our world, but this trip really stretched us.

Several months later, back in the USA, we received an invitation from Costas and his wife Effthelia to attend a party they were hosting in Athens. I immediately thought,

"If we have to sell the house we are going". Costas then added, "And when Costas invites you, I pay for everything!" "Everything" included first class tickets on Swiss Air, being picked up by Costas in his Jaguar, hotel, and meals! It was truly amazing. The party was another pooling of intriguing people. They flew Sharin Isban, the classical guitarist who had just performed at Carnegie Hall, to play in what had been Effthalia's family home in Kolonaki. It was a large white Kykladic home filled with exquisite art. Her father had been ambassador for Greece in China. One lovely and delicate Chinese statue of a spirited horse stands out in my mind still. In a vase on the floor on the evening of the festivities were brilliant red roses with the longest stems I had ever seen; they were as tall as a piano. We were all seated in a large living room and I felt like I was transported back into another century. There were large bowls of caviar that had just been flown from Russia, and fine champagne. I found Effthalia to be an elegant, charming, and intelligent woman who specialized in restoring and studying icons.

After the party Frank had to return to his job. I was currently teaching art classes and I informed my students, "You will see me when you see me". I stayed on in Greece and for our anniversary Frank gave me a week on the boat we had cancelled the previous holiday. On the boat there happened to be seven artists. We sailed between Tinos, Mykonos, Delos, Ios, Santorini, and Paros. We sketched and painted and I also felt moved to write some poetry as well. Greece was such a muse. I felt all my senses exploding and becoming alive on a new level. The landscape was raw and exciting.

We sailed between Paros and Antiparos as the sun began to set. The coral and yellow colours were rich and vibrant as they faded into the sea. We docked in Parokia as the sun set. I froze the moments. I went with Gregory our guide to Yria to select a plate for his father, and on to the Balcony for dinner. The next day we went to Naoussa. It was the most picturesque fishing village I had ever laid eyes on. It had no boutiques then and was quite uncommercial except for a simple shop selling seashells. I took two rolls of film in Naoussa alone. On the way back to our vessel I witnessed my first wheat-threshing with a donkey circling an aloni. After experiencing the strength and masculinity of Santorini, Paros felt so feminine and gentle. I remember thinking, "I could live here."

When I returned to New Jersey my creativity exploded. I painted and wrote. I told Frank that I needed to spend more time in Greece to paint. I was so deeply affected by the culture, the people, and the land and sea. Frank quickly responded, "Sure, you can do that." I bounced back with, "Well a couple months would be great." He again said, "Why not?" I promptly came back, "Actually six months would be ideal!"
"Well, if it is that long, I want to go too," Frank replied. Greece had also touched him profoundly.

Around this time I suggested that we do an exercise I used with corporate executives when I worked as a management consultant. I gave us each a piece of paper and I said, "pretend you are eighty-five looking back on your life. What would you regret if you hadn't been it, done it, or experienced it?" We wrote separately and prayed there would be something the same on our lists. We had three things in common. 1. Simplify our busy lives. 2. Get closer to nature. 3. Live in a foreign country. We realized going to Greece would give us all three. We began discussing how we could break out of the rat race and follow our hearts. We plotted our escape from the American Dream as we decided we would go for a whole year. This meant quitting our jobs since there was no sabbatical, renting our home, and storing our pared-down possessions.

So many thought we were crazy; we had the dream home, two sports cars, and holidays. But we looked at the people at the top of Frank's company where he was a lawyer.

 Yes, they made a lot of money, had great houses but they had little time with their families, and were they truly happy? What was the price for this type of success? These rats wanted out of the race. We opted to go now while we had our health at the young age of thirty-seven. So often, when people wait until retirement to live a dream, one or both of the couple aren't healthy enough. We also wanted to experience Greece before it changed too much. We wanted to see the old women in black sitting on the white-washed steps making lace and sharing the latest gossip. We desired to watch people riding donkeys to the village or to their gardens to tend their vines and olive trees. We wanted to stomp the grapes for wine. Our motto became, "Life isn't a spectator sport!"

We bought our plane tickets for the first of April and drove to Texas to say good-bye to our families. We found Frank's father very ill and his doctor pronounced that he would be gone within a year from cancer. We knew immediately we would stay and take care of him, which we did. It was such a privilege to be disengaged from our normal life so we could help him pass, surrounded with love and as much comfort as possible. Frank settled the estate after the funeral and we were now into August 1986. We were changed by the death of his father, especially when his sister tried to kill us with poison. That story has enough material for a whole book in itself!

We changed our plans yet again and backpacked around the world for nearly a year, ending at last in Greece in June '87. I wanted Frank to feel Paros before we chose which island to settle on. We took the same Viking Star boat I had previously sailed and visited six islands. Frank agreed with me once he experienced Paros: this is it! We moved to Paros on our 17th anniversary and went to dinner at Christos in Naoussa to celebrate. We searched for a yearly rental, which was tough since we kept getting quotes on a daily basis. Then we were led to the tiny kokinou spiti at Agia Irini.

We rented it from the wonderful Alakesto family. It was no longer red, and consisted of two tiny rooms with nonexistent toilet facilities and no running water. Frank had to run across the dirt road to fetch our water from a well. We made an outside shower with a suspended trashcan. When we met Bishop Timothy he announced that he recognized us because he could see us showering from his home up the hill. Oops! The kitchen consisted of a gas bottle with an attached burner that we stuck in the small corner fireplace. We made furniture from the wooden crates that were thrown away when the medical equipment was unpacked for the then-new clinic for the island. We painted the boxes different shades of blue and turquoise and added bright red curtains hung on string. We made it HOME and we were in love with our spirit spiti. It was also exciting to finally unpack the backpacks after a year of hauling them around. We celebrated each sunset and were mesmerized by the night skies. We swam and snorkeled daily. We watched the full moon set behind Antiparos if we woke up early enough. I don't think I've known greater joy in any home. We had done it - we were living our dream. Later in the year, as winter set, in we found a more substantial rental home. When we first saw it we knew it was the home for us as we spotted a couple making love on the roof! But, we kept renting our beloved spirit spiti for another year and went often. During that year we decorated it with purple bougainvillea and roses for a honeymoon "suite" for special friends, John and Jane.

Our one year expanded and became nearly ten. We sold our home in the States and eventually bought the more substantial rental home in which I live now overlooking the bay of Naoussa. We made Paros our home. We continued to surround ourselves with images, and experiences that we loved about Greek living. We celebrated the season changes. The riot of colour during spring as the fields dazzled us bursting with yellow daisies and poppies with their bright red lanterns of light. We made wreaths on May first. There was the heady atmosphere of summer days filled with hazy sunshine.

We learned to appreciate the chirping sounds of cicadas. In the fall we picked our own olives and hauled them to the press and felt great satisfaction with the golden elixir. We helped the men of the soil pick grapes and we stomped them for wine. From our rooftop we studied the heavens with the use of a purchased star book and telescope. We had meteor parties to watch the shooting stars streak across the sky. Some had tails of amazing colours. Scintillating stars with flickering colours as the star entered the atmosphere low on the horizon became a normal sight. The days were punctuated with the sounds of goat bells and the flurry of doves in flight. The landscape was filled with the scent of wild sage, thyme and oregano. Freedom of body and spirit was experienced on remote nude beaches. Candles were lit in exquisite Greek Orthodox churches decorated with silver and gold framed icons as well as very simple and tiny family chapels. It was refreshing to spend time with people that never asked what you did for a living or had done. One was valued for what one was as a person, not for what one had or did. We bonded into a community of wonderful people that became family by choice. We pulled together and supported each other when there was a need or a celebration was in order.

Our lives were so much more simplified than in the States. We washed clothes by hand for years. We finally purchased a used washing machine that we had on the terrace. The first time we used it we pulled up a couple of chairs and with wine watched the clothes turning through the window of this amazing device that most take for granted. We were on a waiting list for eight years to get a telephone, which is hard to imagine with all the cell phones now. I recall not even hearing a phone ring for a whole year. Our social gatherings were always potluck and simple affairs. Many things weren't available on the island then. There is one memory that stands out: we were traveling for a visit to the States and I asked Jane, a good friend, if I could get her anything. She said she desperately needed a new potholder. She showed me her worn and tattered remnant.

Before I left, I gave her my old one that looked a bit better than hers to use until I returned; from her reaction you would have thought I had given her a gold bracelet!

Reminiscing, more precious memories float to the surface. I learned from the Greeks to mix all ages. We would go to a party and eighty-year olds would be dancing with small children. In many cultures the generations become segregated, but not here. We can learn so much from the other age groups. I love how the Greeks don't have to be perfect to dance, sing, or play an instrument. In America we are programmed that one must be perfect before we would dare share with others. But here they sing or dance from their heart and soul to express, not impress. A good example was Chris, who played the flute at Pethaludes. He had just obtained a used clarinet in Athens and came to share his excitement with us. He squeaked and squealed as he blew into the instrument, but it was wonderful. He brought joy to us, if not fine music.

There was the special experience of entering the then working windmill outside of Lefkes. I can still hear the whirling sounds of wooden cog wheels turning, circles within circles. The canvas sails were somewhat torn and patched from use in strong winds. The old man complained that there was no one that wanted to take over the mill that had been in the family for generations. I insisted on having some rather rough ground wheat, which he wanted to continue to sift. I made some biscuits that were beyond textured. Talk about roughage; there were bits of straw sticking out.

Of course we had to celebrate Thanksgiving Day while here. At that time the butcher didn't sell turkey. We learned of a farmer that would sell us one. We drove to the farm to pick it up. He brought out a live bird! "Oh no, you must kill it for us," we pleaded and for an additional cost he did. We took it home and got out the wonderful cookbook *The Joy of Cooking*. It actually explained how to gut and clean the creature.

When the job was complete, the turkey seemed way too small to feed the twenty guests that were invited. We roasted a few chickens and put the herd on the table. Flexibility is the key to happiness.

We had some interesting experiences with the Greek language. During our first winter we wanted to order firewood. We got out the Greek- English dictionary and memorized what to say. In Margarita's shop in Naoussa we spewed out our request for a small boatload of firewood to keep us warm in the winter. Well, that is what we thought we were saying. Evidently, our eye slipped a line in the dictionary and we were asking for a boatload of fireworks to keep us warm! Another time, a Greek woman told us it was her birthday and Frank tried to say that he had just had a birthday. What he announced was that he had given birth the week before! The old woman burst into gales of laughter.

Greece had poignantly provided the answer to the three things we wanted in common before we died. We had simplified our lives, gotten closer to nature and lived in a foreign country! But, unfortunately after nearly ten years we needed to leave our semi-retirement and return to the US to earn some money. It was difficult to leave Paros, but we kept our home and rented it. We gathered our precious memories and returned to America. Thank goodness we had followed our hearts when we did. Frank died of lung cancer within a few years after turning a mere fifty-one. He was rare in that he died with no regrets; he had lived a full and rich life. If we had been practical and waited to live our dream, Frank wouldn't have seen the world or lived in our adopted country which he loved with all his heart and soul, as I do. My body was born in Alabama, but my spirit was born in Greece where I now reside on Paros full-time. Here, I am filled with vibrations that can only be felt in places, which captivate one's soul.

Gail Saunders, Paros, Greece, May 2012.

The owner picked up our table with all the dishes and glasses using only his teeth!
Courtesy of Gail Saunders

SUZANNE'S STORY · 1987
By Suzanne Rolland

Suzanne in Aliki 1987

"Room, room, looking for a room?"

From my apartment in Montreal, Canada, during the winter of 1986, I carefully planned a trip to the Greek Islands for the following summer. I knew that I wanted to do some island-hopping alone with a small packsack. I decided to start with three islands and spend one week in each of them. The Cyclades islands were first on my list and I chose Folegandros, Santorini and Paros after reading various travel guides. Folegandros, they suggested, was a smaller island, Santorini attracted more tourists, while Paros had a more human dimension and a description that appealed to me! I landed first on Santorini by plane from Athens and was fascinated by its sensational sunsets and fabulous landscapes; then I took a ferry to Folegandros where its natural beauty, tiny and beautiful Chora and a very welcoming population amazed me. After two weeks in Greece, I was really looking forward to my next visit to the island of Paros.

The hotel

I arrived on Paros by ferry from Folegandros with my camera on one shoulder and my packsack on my back. Coming off the boat, I saw a group of Greek men screaming at us, the tourists, hoping we would look at their advertisement for room rentals, signs for guest houses, showing us photos and distributing leaflets. One of them pointed to a photo album asking me if I wanted a room. "Ne", I answered. "Posso?" I asked. He gave me a price. I said "Ohi, too much money." I asked where his small hotel was. He pointed to the bay at the end of the harbor. I said too much money again and he laughed. I added with a smile that his photos were not the best I had seen and did not even show that his hotel was located on the seaside. He laughed again and asked me if I took nice photos, pointing at my camera. I nodded. He then added, "you do good photos for me, I give you good price for a room."

We shook hands and off I went following him to his green minivan. This was my first encounter with Giorgos and my introduction to Paros and I loved it. As I was waiting for him to get other tourists, I thought I was in a good place, both mentally and physically, taking the time to look around at the harbor, the sea and the houses. The sky was as blue as the sea, the sun was in its full dress outfit and the harbor was busy with cars, scooters, trucks, people, dogs and we were parked next to a small chapel with the bluest dome I had ever seen. So lovely.

At the hotel I was taken to a small bedroom with a balcony overlooking the sea. I sat there for a while admiring the view after unpacking when I heard Giorgos inviting me to join him and his wife in the garden. I was introduced to Efy, who later became a friend, and was offered a glass of ouzo while fish were being barbecued. We had a nice meal of mezze, a Greek salad and a few grilled fish while sharing information about who we were. They were curious, like all the people I had previously met as to why I was traveling alone. We talked about their hotel and the photos I would take the next day at sunset. I went to bed thinking how wonderful my first day on Paros had been, as making contact with people was always on top of my list to define a great place.

The photos

The next afternoon, Giorgos took me out on his fishing boat into the middle of Livadia bay so I could take pictures of the sea with the hotel in the background. We "put putted" slowly around while I was taking photos from all kinds of angles to get the best shots. I then took some from my balcony, the garden area, the bar and the restaurant in the front. I had the film rolls developed in town and Giorgos was very pleased with the result and, yes, I was given a very good price for my room. After a few days my photos were used to introduce the hotel to future clients off the ferries. Giorgos later sold his hotel so now I don't know what happened to that photo album.

On my last trip to Paros in 2010, I could see that the surroundings in Livadia had changed to a more modern look with sidewalks, cafes and more tavernas and that the Greek men, and now also a few women, were still selling their rooms and hotels to tourists off the boat but were now kept outside the harbor area.

The job offer

During the week, Giorgos asked me if I would take photos of Mr. Mitsodakis, one of the candidates for the next election for the position of Prime Minister of Greece, who was coming to Paros for a political rally. I was given an official scarf with the colors of the Nea Demokratia Party and a written pass to access the site where the helicopter would land on the harbor. Off I went for the day taking shots of the crowd following the candidate around town. I stood on the steps of the podium for his speech; I walked Giorgos and my pictures ended up in the local newspapers and were sent to the party's headquarters in Athens. Funny moments for a French Canadian woman landing on Paros for the very first time.

Agaria

One morning, I walked into an art gallery in the pedestrian streets of Paroikia and heard French being spoken by the owners. I introduced myself in French and we had a good talk as they were getting their place ready for the 10am opening. I asked Elyzabeth and Jacques where I should go on Paros and they recommended the small village of Agaria with a walk down to the beach of Aliki, a lovely fishing village they really enjoyed. I did not know then that I was in for an unforgettable   meeting with a lovely Greek family and that I would fall in love with Aliki, which would become my Greek home for the next twenty years. In fact, I was so happy with my whole day that I later went back to the art gallery with a small bottle of ouzo and some pistachios to thank the couple for their suggestions. We met for a late dinner that night and became friends over the years. After a nice breakfast at the hotel, I took a bus to Agaria and I asked a Greek woman sitting beside me if Agaria was far from Paroikia. She had a hard time understanding what I meant but with a lot of gestures and some laughs she figured it out and showed a few fingers to indicate how many kilometers away was my destination. She pointed to the door as we approached the village and got off the bus with me. I started to look around when I heard her say "elado, elado," looking at me and gesturing me to follow her. I did.

She introduced me to Michaelis, her husband, and told me her name was Victoria Ragoussis. I sat in her kitchen and we started talking: her with words, me with signs and we understood each other and laughed. She was curious about me, a woman traveling alone. "Isse moni?" was the question I was asked. I showed photos of my family with my two sons, my husband, my house in Montreal; she took me outside to see her garden where she picked some tomatoes, got fresh eggs, cut some onions. We walked back to the kitchen and she started cooking a huge omelet with feta and bread. I thought she was making breakfast for her husband when I realized it was all for me. I could not tell her I just had a huge breakfast in Paroikia! Victoria opened the shutters and screamed something to the neighbors. Three women showed up, sat around the kitchen table with their knitting and crochet work and greeted me with a smile and a kalimera. Victoria explained, in Greek, our meeting on the bus, told them who I was, that I came from Canada and that I was traveling alone. Again I heard the Greek word moni. The women addressed me in Greek, I tried to answer in the few Greek words I knew and Victoria repeated what I just tried to say. I realized she was very proud to have a foreigner sitting in her house. So I started addressing her and she would then speak to the women, translating what I told her; she even explained the photos of my family, my children and my apartment in Montreal. This three-way conversation went on for two hours when I realized it would not be too impolite for me to leave. I got up with a lot of efkaristos and yassas and Victoria took me to the front door with a basket packed with a full lunch to take to the beach since I had said I would walk down to Aliki to spend the rest of the day on the beach. We hugged and kissed and I promised to come by again before I left the island. The next morning I walked into the Paroikia post office asking for Kostas, as Victoria had explained that one of her sons was working there. He knew immediately who I was! He was charming, welcoming me to the island, thanking me for going to his mum's house, explaining that she never had a tourist in her house before and that she felt very possessive of me and had so much enjoyed meeting me. Each time I went back to Paros, I would take the bus to Agaria to see Victoria and her family and bring her a small gift from Montreal. I always left her house with fresh vegetables and eggs from her garden. Her son Kostas and his wife invited me a few times over the years into their beautiful house in Agaria, Victoria's son-in-law installed the ceramic tiles on the floor in my house and her daughter invited me to see her place when she was getting married. Years later when I bought my little spiti in Aliki, Victoria and her family would come around to visit me. The Ragoussis will forever be in my heart, in fact I still hear from Kostas via emails from time to time.

Aliki

Upon my first visit, following Victoria's instructions to reach Aliki, I walked down the road with my basket until I arrived at a small kiosk near a lovely beach by a children's park with benches under some pine trees. I sat there observing the activities with the fishing boats moving in the wind on their anchors, children running about in the sand, women standing in the water chatting in a circle with water up to their shoulders. I started taking photos, enjoying the peaceful moment. There was a cafe-taverna at the beginning of a small road along the sea and I thought it was time for a coffee. I had eaten so much food that morning but had declined the Greek coffee offered at Victoria's house. So now the craving could not be neglected any longer. I had discovered the frappes on that trip and was really hooked on them.. I decided then, before sitting down for coffee, to walk along the promenade by the sea all the way to another long narrow beach, empty of houses and people, with dogs wading in the water to cool off. I made Piso Aliki, one of my favorite beaches in Aliki, when I settled in the village a few years later.

At the cafe, I was greeted with a kalimera and I ordered, in Greek, a "frappe, sketo me gala, parakalo." Of course, with the help of my Berlitz dictionary, I had learned a few words: kalimera, efkaristo, parakalo, kalinicta, yassou, pou ine toiletta, ouzo me mezze, all basic small sentences. They always got me a few smiles from the Greek people and I usually got answers. I still remember the taste of my first frappe at what is now called

Manolis Taverna and I will never forget the hour I just spent there, sitting on the edge of the sidewalk, observing life around me. It was at that precise moment that I told myself, this is it! This is where I want to retire! This is where I want to park myself in Greece! I decided that here, in this village which I still had not visited, t I will buy a place! It happened in 1987 and I went back to Aliki, either for a few weeks or a few months, year after year, until I finally bought in 1992. I never missed a year on Paros from 1987 until 2008 when I sold the house.

The decision

In 1990, things in my private life changed; I divorced my husband of twenty-five years and later met the man with whom I would share my life for the next eighteen years. A week after our first meeting though, I left him temporarily for my yearly stay on Paros. My new companion, Godfrey, had never been to Greece so the following year he came with me and understood my passion for Paros. In fact, his first reaction was to tell me he would go half and half with me if I ever found my dream place in Aliki. One year later, I did. It all started with a request to a Greek friend in Montreal if she knew anyone on Paros who could help me find a house. Her aunt was living in Paroikia and she was very happy to help. She introduced us to a real estate agent who said he had three apartments for us to visit. I will always remember my reactions when we approached the first place. Driving on a small dirt road, he pointed to a little white house with blue shutters and a small veranda. My eyes filled up with tears as I said to both men in the car: this is exactly what I wanted; it is what I saw in my dream. I could not believe it. The agent told us that upstairs and downstairs were for sale and he gave us both a set of keys telling us to take the rest of the afternoon to look inside and walk the area. We were invited to meet him at his office in Paroikia later that day to return the keys and, if we did not like any of those two places, he would take us to the third one he wanted us to see. During the day, the two of us discussed the pros and cons of each apartment and took time to explore both places and we also walked to the nearest beach in seven minutes, which was an added bonus for us. But we realized the place needed some renovations and lots of work in the garden and we should take that into account if we were to make an offer. By the end of the day, we preferred the upstairs apartment and agreed to make an offer if the price was close to what we had in our mind and in our bank accounts.

The drama

I was so thrilled to realize this was the place I really wanted that I did not want to visit anything else. We decided to make an offer for the upstairs as soon as we arrived at the real estate office. The price was affordable for both of us and our offer was accepted after a few discussions and negotiations. I clearly remember asking why the agent was not calling the owner to make sure our offer would be accepted. Well, the owner was in fact the agent but he had not wanted to tell us so that we could negotiate without feeling embarrassed to do so with him. He immediately told us that we did not have to wait for the transfer of funds and the notary papers to be signed before moving into the apartment. He added: "why should you pay for a hotel room when you could immediately start enjoying your new place." We did not hesitate to accept his offer as we learned that both apartments were usually rented so they were all furnished and equipped for cooking and sleeping. Waiting for all official papers to be ready, I remember Godfrey laughing as he was cleaning the fridge and stove during that week and telling me that if the deal did not go through, at least the owner would have a cleaner place to rent! My God, I could not believe it when we arrived at the notary's office. Twelve persons were sitting in the room: previous clients stayed to watch, the next group of people were curious so they had arrived earlier, an official translator was introduced as a retired general from the Greek army and the nephew of my Greek friend's aunt. Because he spoke French and English very well, he had been asked to translate all the papers we were about to sign. Angelos and Reena would become our mentors and very good friends over all the years we have been on the island. Of course, also in the room, were two lawyers, some witnesses, the seller, we two buyers, the aunt, the notary and her staff and a secretary. It seemed to us that they were talking very loud and all at the same time as we were both trying to understand what was going on. Of course, we had previously been to the tax office for the official stamps and to the bank to get the drachmas in cash in a brown paper bag and we produced all those necessary papers. It felt like we were at the zoo not realizing that the real drama was still to come. All of a sudden, the female notary started screaming at us in Greek. Our translator told us she was looking for the deed of the property and could not find it in our papers. This was all news to us as we had thought that this had been done by the other lawyer! So we had to tell our translator that we did not have those papers in our possession. Wow, a lot of fast-talking and loud screaming started and we were almost on the verge of leaving and forgetting the whole project. Everybody calmed down when the seller offered to help a lawyer whom our translator knew and who would be available to do the research quickly as we were leaving for Montreal four days later. So we apologized for our lack of knowledge, agreed on another rendezvous for the following Monday and went out feeling like two sheep ready to be killed for an Easter lunch! This is where Angelos took over our misery, calling his lawyer friend to meet us for lunch and treating us to a full mezze meal with ouzo. He laughed as he said: "Suzanna, welcome to the Greek bureaucracy, adding, don't worry, all will be done in time, I know this agent, he is a good man and will have all his papers in order." Well, he did. The lawyer quickly obtained all the required papers and we signed, with a lot less people to watch us, twenty-four hours before we boarded a plane, mentally exhausted, relieved and so, so, so happy. It was the 23rd of June 1992 and we went with Angelos, our official and very patient translator, along with his wife, to eat a meal in the small platia's taverna under the pine trees in the village of Kostos. There was a huge bonfire with all the young children jumping the fire while the adults were watching. I also jumped over the burning wood as I was so excited to finally be the owner of a small one-bedroom apartment in this Greek island. But, as often with Greek people, we could not invite our new friends for dinner as earlier arrangements had been made by Angelos as to who would invite who for that meal and pay for it. We looked at each other and promised to return the favor with a full meal in our new house the following year upon our return.

We celebrated the moment and toasted to a good day with a great finale. I slept in our little spiti that night hugging Godffrey, so excited about our journey.

The conclusion

It is definitively the people of Paros, with their sense of hospitality, friendliness and warmth, who made the difference in choosing this island to start another life. Yes, the many Greeks and foreigners I met during all my trips to Paros were certainly the main factor in deciding to put down some small roots in this beautiful island. And to top it all, it was love at first sight with Aliki, with the beaches in and around the village, with my daily walks where my dog would run free on the path along the sea from Makria Miti to Voutakos, with the small family tavernas, with the lovely little harbor. I even had my secret paradise beach, as I would call it. Few friends were invited to spend a day in my paradise, my very private nudist beach, so close to home. I will forever be grateful to life and, why not, to the Greek Gods, for giving me time to live such a great life on Paros.

Like I always say when I am asked why I bought my spiti on Paros, I always give the same answer: because I was Greek in another life and probably a Pariani Greek and that is why I adopted Paros! Or is it that Paros adopted me?

Suzanne Rolland
Montréal, Canada
December 31st, 2011

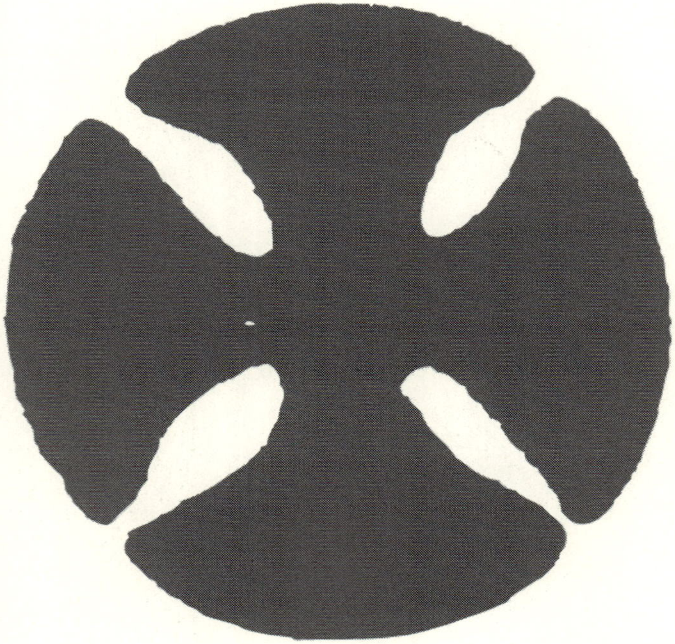